3000 DEGREES

3000 DEGREES

THE TRUE STORY
OF A DEADLY FIRE
AND THE MEN WHO FOUGHT IT

Sean Flynn

WARNER BOOKS

An AOL Time Warner Company

This book is based on the author's "The Perfect Fire," which appeared in *Esquire* magazine July 2000.

Warner Books, Inc., 1271 Avenue of the Americas, New York, NY 10020

Visit our Web site at www.twbookmark.com.

 An AOL Time Warner Company

Printed in the United States of America

First Printing: March 2002

10 9 8 7 6 5 4 3 2 1

ISBN: 0-446-52831-5
LCCN: 2002101313

Text design by Stanley S. Drate / Folio Graphics Co. Inc.

For Louise

Acknowledgments

In the beginning, which was December 1999, there was David Granger, who is the editor of *Esquire* magazine. He told me about watching, with tears in his eyes, a memorial service for six firemen who had died inside an old warehouse in Worcester, Massachusetts. Yet as tragic as the specific event had been, he recognized—and asked me to write about—the deeper themes involved: the courage, loyalty, and honor among men who risked their lives for one another. The story he wanted was less about one fire than about the dozens of men who fought it and the thousands of others like them in small towns and big cities who would have done the same.

David had to wait six months for that story, but he was patient. He assigned Andy Ward, the finest editor working in magazines, to help me shape it, and Luke Zaleski, a dogged researcher, to check each of the facts. And the final product, which was published in July 2000, became the frame upon which this book was eventually built. For all of that, David, I am extremely grateful.

There were others, of course, who helped along the way. Early on, Dr. John A. Greene, a psychologist who specializes in counseling firefighters, guided me into their subculture, made introductions, vouched for my character, and explained the nuances of a fireman's head. Mike Mullane from the International

Association of Fire Fighters and Frank Raffa and Ed Ryan from IAFF Local 1009 opened my first doors into the Worcester Fire Department. Their assistance was invaluable and appreciated.

My agent, David Black, has provided wise counsel and unwavering support, which makes him as fine a friend and ally as any man deserves. My editor, Rick Horgan, taught me how to craft a mountain of facts into a long and proper narrative. It would be difficult to overstate either of their contributions.

During months of writing, a number of people accomodated me in one way or another. John Gearan of the Worcester *Telegram & Gazette* and Charles P. Pierce, a Worcester native and gifted writer, both tried to explain their city to me. Luke Zaleski signed on for the daunting task of checking each of the facts that follow. Suzi Samowski and her staff at Bukowski Tavern never once complained when I hogged the corner table and asked for a fresher pot of coffee. Ted Miller and Bernadette Carr were irreplaceable confidants. Brekke Fletcher, Liz Wallace, and Ingrid Eberly indulged my rougher passages and offered their sage advice. And Louise Jarvis blessed me with her insight, her companionship, and her tolerant love.

None of these words would have been written, however, without the cooperation of scores of people in Worcester. Denise Brotherton, Mary Jackson, Michelle Lucey, Jim and Joan Lyons, Linda McGuirk, and Kathy Spencer were all exceedingly generous with their time and their memories. So, too, were dozens of firemen, too many to mention by name but many of whom appear in the following pages. I am indebted to all of them, and especially to District Chief Michael O. McNamee. Two years ago, his men told me that they thought Mike was a hero. He would never use that word to describe himself, but it is true. I hope he believes it, and that it brings him some comfort.

3000
DEGREES

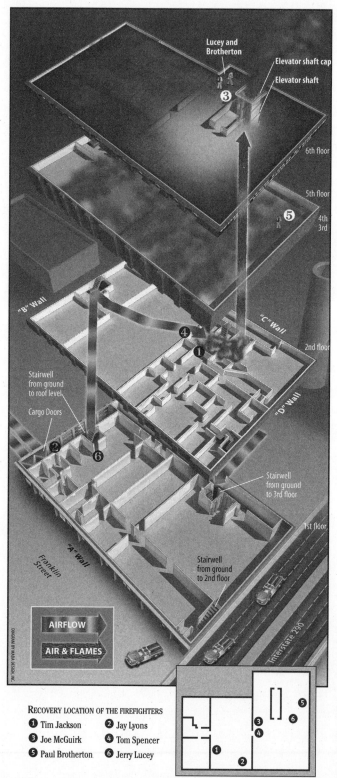

Lucey and
Brotherton

Elevator shaft cap

Elevator shaft

❸

6th floor

5th floor

❺

4th
3rd

"B" Wall

"C" Wall

❹

❶

2nd floor

Stairwell
from ground
to roof level

"D" Wall

Cargo Doors

❷

❻

Stairwell
from ground
to 3rd floor

Stairwell
from ground
to 3rd floor

1st floor

"A" Wall

Franklin
Street

Stairwell
from ground
to 2nd floor

Interstate 290

AIRFLOW

AIR & FLAMES

DIAGRAM BY MAJA DESIGN, INC.

RECOVERY LOCATION OF THE FIREFIGHTERS

❶ Tim Jackson   ❷ Jay Lyons

❸ Joe McGuirk   ❹ Tom Spencer

❺ Paul Brotherton   ❻ Jerry Lucey

❶ The fire started sometime between 4:30 and 6 p.m. on December 3, 1999, when a candle tipped onto a pile of clothing in a makeshift bedroom on the second floor.

❷ At 6:15, two minutes after the first alarm was struck for a fire at Worcester Cold Storage, men from Ladder 1 and Rescue 1 forced open a door on the loading dock.

❸ At about 6:18, after climbing the stairs on the B wall and breaking through a bulkhead on the roof, Paul Brotherton and Jerry Lucey vented the building by smashing out a glass skylight covering an elevator shaft. The hole in the roof, fifteen-feet by fifteen-feet, allowed smoke and hot air to escape.

❹ At 6:20, Stephen "Yogi" Connole and John Casello found the fire on the second floor. While waiting for hoses to be brought up and charged, Yogi wrestled to keep the door closed. With fresh air flowing from the B side of the building and hot air blowing up through the C-side elevator shaft, a strong draft pulled the door toward the fire.

For the next twenty-five minutes, firemen flanked the fire, attacking it with hoses threaded up both the B-side stairs and C-stairs. The flames were aggressive, feeding on cool air sucked in from below. At 6:40, a third alarm was struck, dispatching another twelve men to assist the forty-two already battling the fire.

A minute later, at approximately 6:41, the building filled with black smoke, reducing visibility to zero in less than four seconds. District Chief Mike McNamee, choking on smoke in the B stairs, ordered every man down to the first floor for a head count.

❺ At 6:46, Jerry Lucey, who was on the fifth floor with Paul Brotherton when conditions deteriorated, keyed his radio. "Rescue 600 to command," he said. "We need help on the floor below the top floor of the building. We're lost."

Search teams were immediately assembled at the bottom of the B stairs. McNamee ordered men to use safety lines as they crawled into the boiling black on the floors above, feeling for Brotherton and Lucey. Twenty-two minutes after Lucey's first transmission, Lieutenant Tom Spencer radioed from the fifth floor that he and his men were lost. Eight minutes later, he sent a final broadcast. "Ladder 2 to Command," he said. "We're done…"

❻ After searching for more than an hour, Mike McNamee realized the six men were missing and that more might die if he didn't call off the rescue attempt. He stood at the bottom of B stairs, physically blocking his men from pushing past him. "Listen to me," he yelled. "We've already lost six. We're not going to lose anymore." Two minutes before eight o'clock, the building was ordered evacuated.

1

THE SMOKE BANKED DOWN LIKE BOLTS OF BLACK VELVET, HEAVY sheets curling and rolling and folding together. A man could lose perspective in such a cloud, the vapor so dense and oily that it carried a physical weight, like tar, hot and sticky and misted into the air. Through the plastic of his face mask, Lt. Mike McNamee could see a dirty orange glow in the haze, brighter when the smoke puffed one way on a searing updraft, then dimmer when the fog closed again. If he trusted his eyes, which he didn't, the flames might have been forty feet away, or sixty, or maybe only twenty. So he trusted his skin, believed in the warmth pushing through his turnout coat. He was down on all fours, crawling across a wood floor, staying low, ducking under the worst of the heat. Down there, in the coolest inches, he figured the temperature was only 125 degrees, maybe 150. He guessed the fire, burning at the back end of a warehouse storeroom eighty feet deep and half as wide, was about forty-five feet away.

"Lieutenant, you wanna open it up?"

The nozzle man, a lump in the dark barely an arm's reach away, shouted the words. Every man in a firefight had to shout, throw his voice through the mask on his face and the droning thunder of the flames. The sound was muffled, almost slurred to an unpracticed ear.

"Not yet," Mike hollered back. "Let's keep moving. Get up close where we can hit it directly."

There were three of them, creeping across the warehouse floor and dragging a hose two and a half inches in diameter loaded with almost four hundred pounds of water. The nozzle man in front and another firefighter in the rear flanked Mike, the ranking officer that night in 1981 on Engine 4 out of the Worcester Fire Department's Park Avenue station. Mike was young for a lieutenant, just a few months past his thirty-first birthday. With his shallow chin and thin-framed spectacles, he sometimes looked like an English professor, which is what he had wanted to be before he dropped out of college. He had a reputation as being mildly bookish anyway, a man who studied fire, the alchemy of oxygen and heat and fuel, and the choreographed chaos of fire suppression: how and when to attack and vent and retreat. But he also had the sturdy build of a fireman, a solid frame conditioned by years humping up smoky tenement stairs and clambering over flaming roofs with seventy pounds of gear on his back. In almost nine years since he'd joined the fire department in his hometown in the middle of Massachusetts, Mike had helped put out more than a thousand blazes, which wasn't an unusual number for a man working that job in that place in those years.

Worcester in the 1970s and early 1980s was a withered industrial city, a factory town abandoned by factory owners and factory workers. Below downtown, just beyond the interstate overpass, old warehouses stood hollow, their insides gutted except for the trash and scraps that could feed a renegade spark. The hills above the Blackstone Valley were lined with sagging wood-framed triple-deckers, tinder-dry and stacked dense as cordwood. The Main South neighborhood was a sprawling slum of deteriorating tenements and abandoned storefronts. And for most of the decade all of it was on fire, the whole city burning lot by lot and night by night. Frayed wires spit sparks onto carpets and curtains, corroded black pipes leaked gas into antiquated kitchens, drunks passed out with Marlboros between their arthritic fingers. Pyromaniacs, half-crazed or half-witted or both, set light to trash cans and gas station bathrooms and flophouse porches and dry stands of grass. What didn't burn by accident or for sport burned for cash. Arson was epidemic, landlords and investors charring the last scraps of profit from decrepit properties, a depressing number of which were worth more as heavily insured ruins than as cheaply rented apartments or vacant commercial space. Some shifts, it seemed all of Worcester might burn to the ground. In the worst years, an engine crew would routinely fight three fires in a single night, and five wasn't uncommon.

After a decade on the frontlines, a flaming warehouse wasn't a particularly formidable foe. Potentially dangerous, sure. But predictable, not exceptionally different from a hundred other skirmishes Mike had been through. He knew the best attack was in close. A two-and-a-half-inch line sprayed out roughly 250 gallons every minute, enough to wash the life out of most medium-size fires. But if the stream missed the flames, if it fell short and hit nothing but superheated air, all that liquid would atomize, instantly mushroom into steam, blow back and down in a scalding vapor. So he ordered his men, nearly blinded by the smoke and hobbled by the weight of their gear and the hose, to keep inching forward. Another fifteen feet, twenty at the most.

Mike was judging the distance to the flames not just by the heat but also by his fresh memory of the building. This was the second time that night Engine 4, along with three other engines, two ladder trucks, and the rescue squad—the normal complement sent to a working fire—had been dispatched to Jacques Street, a short block of squat brick warehouses and machine shops along the tracks of the Providence and Worcester Railroad. The first alarm for 82 Jacques Street came in just after dinner, when the men in the Park Avenue station were wiping the last drops of gravy from their mustaches and splashing their plates into a sink of sudsy water. Three tones sounded, abrupt and abrasive, electrified burps. Then the dispatcher's deadpan voice from the speaker bolted to the wall: "Engine 2, Engine 4, Engine 5, Engine 10, Ladder 4, Scope 3, Rescue 1, Car 4. Striking Box 1575 for a reported structure fire at 82 Jacques Street."

A dozen men working the third tour out of Park Avenue, four each on Aerial Scope 3 and Engines 4 and 10, were moving before the dispatcher started repeating the assignments, hustling into their turnout gear. Most of them pulled on long boots that rose to the middle of their thighs, just above where the bottom edge of their coats would fall. A few, including Mike, stepped through the legs of newfangled fire-resistant pants and into shorter boots. In less than twelve seconds, every man was on his designated truck. The officers took the seats on the passenger sides of the cabs, where they could yank the air-horn cords and toggle the sirens on and off. On the ride south along Park Avenue, each man except the driver slipped his arms through a fire-resistant coat hung on the back of his seat, the sleeves already laced through the straps of an air tank. When Mike's boots hit the pavement outside the warehouse three minutes after the first tone, all of his men were ready to square off against an inferno.

But there wasn't much of a fire left. When the first flames heated the air to 165 degrees or so, tiny metal plugs melted in the sprinkler heads plumbed through the building, opening the spigots and dropping a heavy shower on the fire. The only thing left for the firemen to do was shut off the main valve to the sprinkler system, soak a few embers, and then track down the owner of the building to tell him to replace his spent sprinkler heads and board up his doors and windows. A quick knockdown. Thirty minutes later, they were back at the station, scrubbing the dinner dishes.

If the fire had been accidental, then the sprinklers had saved the building and protected the men who came with their hoses and axes and ladders. If it had been arson, then it had been merely a setup fire, a prelude to a bigger, more devastating and dangerous blaze. With the sprinkler system disabled, the flames from a second torching could get a jump on the fire crews. In the unimpeded minutes before the fire department's arrival, two or three isolated ignition points could engulf the entire building.

The second alarm for 82 Jacques Street came in three hours after the first, shortly before ten o'clock. Dispatch announced the same unit assignments, and all twelve men at Park Avenue, plus eight more from the Webster Square station and ten out of Central Street, quick-stepped back into their gear and onto their trucks. When Mike hit the pavement the second time, black smoke billowed through the roof and blown-out windows. The second floor was fully involved, a tangle of orange and yellow. A second alarm was struck. Headquarters dispatched another dozen men on two more engines and a third ladder company.

The driver on Engine 4 stayed with the truck, working the controls that regulate the water coming in from the hydrants and pump it out through the hoses. Mike and two of his men grabbed a coil of hose from the bed above the back bumper and lugged it toward a street level door, up a staircase, and into a hallway. From the smoke and the sound, they knew the flames were raging somewhere behind a steel fire door that had rolled shut. Much the way the sprinkler heads had been activated by heat, the fire door had automatically closed when the heat melted a pin that held it open, the idea being to contain the fire to one room.

Mike and his men pulled their plastic masks over their faces, cranked open their air tanks, and rolled back the door. Then they dropped to their knees, ducking below air that might have been 300 degrees at waist height and twice that at head height. At the ceiling, twelve feet above, the temperature was nearly 1,500 degrees, almost as hot as a crematorium. With the hose charged—filled with water sent up by the engine's pump—the three of them crawled into the black folds of smoke. When the last man cleared the fire door, it rolled closed behind him, propped open only a couple of inches by the trailing hose.

They were in forty feet, halfway across the storeroom. "Now?" the nozzle man hollered.

"A little closer," Mike yelled back again. Another ten feet, he thought to himself. Ten more seconds, then we'll hit it.

He shuffled his left knee forward, then his right, keeping one hand on the hose and another on his nozzle man. He moved his left knee again, then stopped short when he saw it: a flicker through the smoke, near the ceiling. Then another, a shimmer that brightened and blossomed into a deep yellow glow, the color of overripe lemons. A bad color signaling a very bad thing, a phenomenon Mike had read and heard about, and even witnessed from a distance. But he'd never been up close, directly in its path, had hoped he never would be. The sound came next, a low rumble through the hiss and snap of the fire, like thunder tumbling across a prairie horizon.

One of his men, maybe both of his men, shouted something,

but the words were swallowed up by the growling near the ceiling. Mike reached for his nozzle man. His hand touched nothing but smoke. He wheeled on one knee, flailing his arm behind him for his other man. Nothing. Above him, the rumble swelled and quickened, a trembling whoosh. The storeroom, a box of thick brick walls closed in by a bulky steel door, had trapped too much heat inside. The gases lingering near the ceiling had reached their ignition temperature, the point at which each tiny particle of smoke and wisp of oxygen turned to fire. Mike, groping at smoke in the dark, realized he was alone in a room about to explode. "Oh, fuck," he muttered.

Then he saw it happen. It started on the back wall, above the fire he'd been inching toward, an orange ball expanding, erupting, blowing across the ceiling. It spread to the walls on either side, covered the width of the room, and spun forward, flames biting into the smoke like a thresher into wheat, spears of fire curling and weaving a few feet above Mike's head. It moved as fast as a breaking wave, washing across the length of the storeroom to the wall blocked off by the door, then plunged to the floor, covering all that ground in three seconds, maybe two.

Mike dropped flat on his back as the flames passed over him, as much by training—always stay low, beneath the heat—as instinct. A man could survive a rollover, but it was one of the most terrible phenomena he would ever witness. The only thing worse would have been a flashover. The physics were similar, gases superheating until they exploded. But where a rollover happened near the ceiling, a flashover happened everywhere at once, every scrap of cloth and stick of furniture and atom of hydrogen instantly exploding into flame. A man on the edge of a room about to flash could take maybe two giant, panicked strides out; a man inside that room was going to die.

In the dark, Mike slid his hands to the end of the hose, found the nozzle, and yanked the lever back. Water tore out like cannon fire, jerking the line, forcing it one way, then another, as if the hose was alive, a serpent fighting to get loose. Mike pinned a length of it beneath his back and clamped the rest between his left arm and rib cage, wrestling until he had the nozzle aimed straight up at the ceiling. For the next fifteen seconds—or it could have been five or fifty, because a man can lose track of time when he's trying not to die—Mike washed the air above him, scattering hundreds of gallons of water into the void. But he wasn't getting wet. None of the water was splashing back down. He knew it was turning to steam, a mist that would eventually settle on him like a searing fog. But 212 degrees of steam was better than 1,500 degrees of fire.

For an instant, the flames receded. The bright orange disappeared in a shroud of black smoke, the air finally cooled enough not to burn. Mike had punctured the fire's flanks, sent it into a temporary retreat, the way an army would fall back to regroup. Except a fire regrouped in only seconds, not hours or days. In one quick motion, Mike slammed the nozzle shut, twisted onto his knees, and started crawling, his shins banging off the floor, his hands slapping along the hose line. He covered forty feet like a sprinter, moving so fast in the dark he smashed his head into the fire door just to the left of the opening where the hose slipped out. He could hear his nozzle man screaming. "Where's Mike? Where the fuck is Mike?" Then he saw two pairs of gloved hands pulling at the fire door, wrenching it open just enough for the lieutenant to scramble into the hallway. It rolled shut behind him.

Mike slumped against a wall. His two men were sitting on the floor, wide-eyed, panting. They hadn't meant to leave him alone—firefighters, good ones, never leave a man alone in a fire, and Mike knew these were good men. They had thought he was bailing out with them. That's what they'd been yelling about, the words Mike couldn't hear over the rumbling of the rollover.

Mike stared at them, his breath coming in great, labored gulps. Finally, he said, "Holy fuck." He stared some more and said it again, hoarse, almost a whisper: *"Fuck."*

From behind the door, he could hear another roar, the sound of the room exploding. If he'd been inside, Mike knew, he'd be dead. He considered that, but only for an instant. "Sometimes you have to bring an extra pair of shorts to work," he liked to say. And that was okay. Every fireman, unless he was a fool, sometimes got scared. But they never expected to die. Because, truth be told, they hardly ever did.

2

THE LATE NOVEMBER SUN SANK BEHIND THE GREEN STEEL
trestle of the interstate and the empty warehouses behind it
and, farther off in the western distance, the forested tops of
stubby mountains that creased the middle of Massachusetts
like a scoliotic spine. Mike steered his Buick into the low, gold
light of the afternoon, squinting behind his thin-framed spectacles when the rays stabbed through breaks in the landscape,
between the squat domed spires of Union Station and the
beams holding up the highway and the narrow gaps separating
the triple-deckers. The few strands of cinnamon left in his silver
hair caught the light, glinted like bronze threads.

"Where are you going?" Joanne asked. She sat next to him,
fidgeting with the visor, trying to block the glare. She was a
small woman, not much more than five feet tall, which put her
face, perfectly round with dimples pressed into her cheeks and
an upturned nose, in the bright gap between the dashboard and
the visor. When she narrowed her eyes, her dimples deepened
and her nose crinkled just below the bridge, the same way as
when she smiled.

"I'm taking Franklin over to Grafton," Mike said. "It's faster."

Joanne shrugged. Mike knew the roads in Worcester better than she did, the back alleys and uncluttered lanes that bypass the arteries clogged with late-afternoon traffic. Firemen knew all the shortcuts, the routes that would shave a few seconds off the race to the flames. After twenty-seven years on the job, working out of stations all over the city, Mike had figured out the shortest path from any point in the city to any other, and committed most of them to memory. He was kind of a geek that way. When he was a younger man, a rookie, Mike would walk the blocks around his first station, Winslow Street, with his toddler daughter strapped to his back, noting the location of every fire hydrant. The police thought it was weird enough that they stopped him once or twice, wanting to know why he was casing the neighborhood. Mike would takes his notes home, spread an oversize map on the living room floor and plot all the hydrants with a black marker. It used to drive Joanne nuts, coming home from her shift at the hospital to find her husband crawling around with a pen, the bed unmade, dishes unwashed, baby Kate burbling on the floor next to him.

Kate was twenty-three now, a college student in Washington, D.C. A vegetarian, wouldn't even eat poultry. In a few days, she would be home for Thanksgiving, which was why Mike and Joanne were driving across the city. There was a Middle Eastern bakery on Grafton Hill that made the finest Syrian bread and the best damned spinach pies in central Massachusetts. Kate would eat spinach pie.

Mike turned left onto Franklin Street, passing under the trestle of Interstate 290 and into the shadows of an old warehouse district. Fifty yards up Franklin, Mike took his right hand off the steering wheel and pointed a thick finger ahead and to the right. "See that building?" he said.

Joanne looked where he pointed. She couldn't have missed

it if she'd tried. Worcester Cold Storage was a colossus of brick and mortar, wide as a city block and more than eighty feet tall. It was actually two buildings, connected by a common wall and laid out like a fat L, but from her angle, a dead-on view of the front from the curb, it looked like a massive cube.

"Yeah," she said. "What about it?"

"It scares me."

Joanne looked again. She'd seen that warehouse a thousand times before and never thought it was particularly spooky. It was a landmark, looming over Worcester just east of downtown for four generations. When she was a child, the blocks around it had rumbled and screeched with trucks and railcars, and the stench of offal and blood and diesel hung close to the ground. Hundreds of men labored in a dozen buildings, carving cattle and hogs into steaks and pork chops, fresh cuts that were stacked in the refrigerated warehouses. The meat cutters, like nearly every other industry in Worcester, had moved out of town by the end of the seventies. The cold storage businesses lingered for a few more years, but by the late eighties they were closed as well, the few windows along one stairwell and in front of the old office sealed with plywood and nails, the steel doors on the loading docks padlocked and chained. All that remained were the shells, monoliths of ocher and russet.

Worcester Cold Storage was the biggest of them all, dominating the abandoned abattoirs and freight depots and, in the shadow of its western wall, a small sliver of a diner called the Kenmore. It even dwarfed Interstate 290, eight concrete lanes that cleaved through the center of the city and passed only a couple dozen yards from the sheer brick facade of the warehouse. If anything, the highway gave it a grander scale; in a fluke of perspective, the guardrails of the eastbound lanes underlined the logo—WORCESTER COLD STORAGE AND WAREHOUSE CO.—painted near the top in giant white letters. Everyone in town knew that building, precisely where it was and what it looked like, if only because no one could avoid passing it in traffic.

"It scares you," Joanne repeated. "Really. Why?"

"No windows."

Mike said it casually, a statement of obscure fact. He wasn't immediately frightened, viscerally afraid, like he was that night on Jacques Street, his heart banging against his ribs, his lungs gasping short, shallow breaths. This fear was pragmatic, an educated projection of potential calamity, like that of an engineer who sees the future collapse of a bridge by looking at its badly drawn blueprints.

Joanne studied the building again, trying to focus it through her husband's eyes, a fireman's eyes. A lot of buildings scared firemen, if only because they had learned to mentally overlay the walls and foundations with heat, smoke, and flames. Civilians looked at a strip mall and saw a dry cleaner, a convenience store, and a deli, separate businesses lined up in a row. Firemen saw one long box divided into individual compartments connected by a single airspace between the roof and the dropped ceilings, a passage for flames to sneak from one shop to the next. Where civilians saw a hospital, firemen saw a couple hundred sick people who would need to be carried out, some tethered to respirators that couldn't be disconnected. A Wal-Mart or a Home Depot, through a fireman's prism, became a stockpile of flammable synthetics and explosive chemicals stored under a roof held up by open-web bar joists, a supporting structure that was light and strong but that in the heat of a fire could collapse in less than ten minutes and with little warning. "If that ever goes up," firemen would say, nodding toward a shuttered mill or a fully occupied high-rise, "I hope I'm not working. *When* it goes up, I hope I'm not on."

Mike had to worry about such buildings. He was a district

chief now, in charge of the entire northern half of the city for his shift; at every working fire, he would be the initial supervisor, deciding how to attack and when to retreat. No fire was routine, but most were predictable and, given enough time and rogue sparks, could be practiced. Hundreds of the city's ubiquitous triple-decker houses had caught fire during the past couple of decades, and the next one to go up probably wouldn't burn much differently than all the others before it.

Worcester Cold Storage was a different beast altogether. The sheer size of it was intimidating. A fire running loose inside had too many places to hide and too many places to spread, wide pastures of littered floors on which to grow and thrive. A small fire, found quickly, could be eliminated. A big fire, one that got a jump on the men and slipped through the hallways and into the elevator shafts, flanking, surrounding, would be impossible to control. Worst of all were the unbroken walls, blank stacks of brick rising from the pavement. The building had been designed to hold in cold, which meant it would also retain heat, tremendous temperatures. That was also why there were so few windows, only a handful for light in one isolated stairwell. With no windows, there would be no easy vents, no way to bleed out the heat and the smoke and the poison.

"I'm telling you," Mike said again, "that building scares me. It scares the shit out of me."

"So hope you never get a fire in there." Joanne patted Mike's leg when she said it. "How many pies should we get?"

Joanne used to worry about Mike, years ago, before Kate was born and he was a rookie and they lived in a rented apartment on Vincent Avenue, two miles from the Winslow Street station. They had the top floor of a triple-decker that sat on a hill overlooking a housing project and, if the wind was blowing a particular way on a hot summer night, it would gather the echo of sirens and carry them into the living room, deposit them right beside her. "Don't you die now," she would whisper to her husband, riding around on the streets below. "Don't you dare die now."

The fear, reflexive and unexpected, always startled her, maybe even embarrassed her. Her mother had always told her, "You don't borrow worry." A fine piece of Irish-Catholic fatalism, but it was true and Joanne knew it. She chased away the dread almost as quickly as it came. Besides, she'd never been afraid of fire, and the sound of a siren was familiar, almost comforting. When she was a little girl, she would chase after fire trucks and police cruisers with her father, following the whooping and the wailing just because they were curious.

She'd done the same thing with Mike, too. When she met him, he was a carpenter, a shaggy college dropout swinging a hammer for nonunion wages. He'd gotten himself on the hiring list for the Worcester Fire Department, but only for practical reasons; fighting fires was a civil service job, secure, recession-proof, paid a good wage. He had no particular passion for the trade, no romantic visions of heroism or jittery cravings for danger. It was just a good job in a bad economy. He was waiting for his appointment to the training academy when Joanne saw the change in him, watched a curiosity swell up inside and ripen into an obsession, stood right next to Mike while he stared into a burning house, mesmerized, tantalized.

It happened on the Fourth of July, 1972. The firebugs all came out on Independence Day, flitting through the summer dusk, setting light to scrub brush and trash cans and the occasional house. Every year, the firemen would lurch around the city, screaming from one hot spot to the next, squirting each tangle of smoldering garbage or tinder-dry grass, stalling every so often at a recalcitrant blaze gnawing at something more substantial, like a car or a shopkeeper's goods.

Mike and Joanne went out to watch pieces of the city burn that night, cruising the streets in his gray Belvedere. At about ten-thirty that night, they stopped on Pleasant Street near the corner of Hudson, where, a few minutes earlier, someone had put a match to the front porch of a triple-decker. One of the residents tried to douse the fire with buckets of water, but the flames quickly climbed the walls, the fire rising on its own heat, finding a hold in the clapboard, then pushing itself higher.

By the time Mike and Joanne parked the car and walked closer, the third floor was engulfed in throbbing orange. The street was splattered with swirls of red and white lights from the fire trucks, and the air had a bitter, ashy sting. Mike and Joanne watched men in heavy coats and rubber boots up to the middle of their thighs spread across the lawns and the street, cranking valves on the pumper trucks, steadying ladders against the smoldering walls, a couple more bounding up the porch stairs and through the front door. Smoke swirled from a third-floor window, balls of black cotton tumbling over each other in a race up to the sky.

A hand poked through the cloud, then a head, then a full torso. A fireman leaned over the sill. A blast of flame erupted behind him, and fire shot over his head in fat, snapping tendrils. "I need a line up here," the man shouted. "C'mon, let's go, I need another fucking line."

Mike stood next to Joanne at the curb, transfixed. He could almost feel the heat on the back of his neck, his ears, taste the smoke in the back of his throat, scratching at his esophagus. "Goddamn," he whispered, "that guy's got tremendous balls." Then he felt a twitch in his gut. Adrenaline. He looked at Joanne. "I could do that," he said.

She looked at him, turned her head away, a trace of a smile on her lips. "I know you could," she said.

"No. Joanne, I can *do* that. I *want* to do that."

She said it again. "I know."

Mike answered his first alarm as a Worcester fireman six months later, clinging to the side of a 1951 Maxim Junior Aerial chugging through a sleet storm at forty miles an hour. A few months after that, almost exactly one year after he'd been hypnotized by the flames on Hudson Street, Mike watched ten people die in an inferno that swept through a flophouse on Main Street, the deadliest fire in the city's history. There were too many others to count, the tenements and factories, the triple-deckers and cheap hotels, where Mike had crawled into the smoke and the flames and walked back out. He'd never even gotten badly hurt. A few bumps and bruises, the occasional blistering burn and tufts of singed hair, and, once, a wrenched spine from the cannon stream of a wayward hose that threw him off a porch and a dozen yards through the air, onto a concrete sidewalk. He missed a few weeks after that one. But he always went back to work.

You don't borrow worry. It was true and Joanne knew it and, in time, she came to believe it.

3

DAWN WAS SILVERY GRAY, LIKE A NEW DIME, MORNING LIGHT glowing through unbroken clouds. It was December 3, 1999, a Friday, and Joe McGuirk was driving southwest toward Charlton, the twilight rising in his rearview mirror. If he hurried, he could put in five hours, maybe six, frame a stack of two-by-fours into skeletal walls, and still get home to Linda by noon.

Joe didn't build many houses. He preferred remodeling jobs, putting in new kitchens and bathrooms, self-contained projects where he could handle most of the work himself, not have to hire any labor. He was the sole proprietor of McGuirk & Son Construction, which was something of a misnomer because his only son was just ten years old. Joe liked the name, though. He'd been calling his company that since 1989, the year he got his contractor's license and the same year Everett was born. "And Son," Joe had reasoned, made his outfit sound bigger, older, more established. And it wasn't technically untrue.

He was a self-taught carpenter. An electrican and plumber and mechanic, too. If it could be hammered, sawed, bolted, wired, screwed, caulked, Joe could figure it out. He might get zapped eight times trying to fix a busted switch with the power connected, but he got the lights to work. Linda believed he could do anything, because she'd never seen him not be able to do something. When he was younger, he worked as a handyman at the Jewish Community Center, where he met a lot of people who wanted their peeling Victorians painted. He did that for a few years, studying at night for his contractor's license and practicing on the four-room bungalow he and Linda bought before they got married. He gutted every room, fixed it up nice, then built a second story on top. After that, he blew out the back wall, added another room, ripped out the kitchen again, put in a new one, then remodeled it a third time. With the additions, the deck, and the garage, he'd built on every inch of their property by the early nineties. So he found a new piece of land, out in the woods in Rochdale, in the wooded valleys southeast of the city, and started over. He worked for hours, absorbed in the labor, the headlights from his truck illuminating the joists and the columns he pieced together on his own. He framed the entire thing, twenty-five hundred square feet, in two weeks. (Joe did everything fast; he jogged behind the lawnmower.) He painted the clapboards pink and bolted green shutters to the windows and moved in with Linda, Everett, and Emily, his little girl, five years earlier, right before Thanksgiving in 1994.

Funny how it worked out, Joe making a living building things, and still making a good buck at it even though it was only a side job. He started contracting because he couldn't get on the Worcester Fire Department. He'd always wanted to be a fireman, like his dad, Wild Bill McGuirk, and his big brother Billy. He took the damned test every chance he got since his senior year in high school. Scored pretty well, too, way up in the high nineties. But something always got in the way at hiring time. In the early eighties, it was affirmative action, the city trying to hire more minorities in a department dominated by white guys. Some years, the budget was too tight. Mostly, though, it was the military veterans who kept edging him out: a man who came out of the army moved to the top of the hiring list if he passed the test. So Joe would score a ninety-seven and lose out to a vet with a ninety-three.

In the summer of 1995, after fifteen years of frustration, Joe realized he needed an act of God, or at least the state legislature, to make him a fireman. He talked to a friend, a city councillor named Wayne Griffin. Wayne liked Joe, had known his family forever. Joe built the deck on the back of Wayne's house, hammered his campaign signs together, stood on a corner holding one on Election Day. Wayne explained a home-rule petition to him, how the state could make a law that would give him preference on account of his father having been a fireman. It would have to pass the city council and the house of representatives and then the governor would have to sign it, but it could be done.

A few days later, Joe told Linda, "I'm going to Boston. I'm going to see the governor."

"Cut the shit," Linda said.

"No, really. I'm going to see the governor. I gotta do something."

Joe drove to Boston, up to Beacon Hill, staked out Gov. William Weld. He caught up to him in an elevator. "Governor, my name is Joe McGuirk," he said, just blurted out the words. "My father, Bill McGuirk, was a Worcester fireman and he died in the line of duty and I've been trying to get on the job for fifteen years, since 1980, I keep taking the test and getting good scores but I'm always a couple of points short because I don't get the preference from my dad having been on the job so I wanted to try a home-rule petition and what do you think?"

Weld stood there for a moment, not saying anything. Then he grinned. "I like you," he told Joe. "You get the bill on my desk and I'll sign it."

Wayne wrote it up, convinced the city council to pass it, sent it along to the statehouse. The house passed it and, in November 1995, Weld signed it. There it was, in black and white, Chapter 197 of the Acts and Resolutions of 1995. "An Act Relative to Civil Service Preference of Certain Members of the Family of William T. McGuirk for Appointment to the Fire Department of the City of Worcester." His very own law. He had to wait almost two more years before the city hired him, at the beginning of September 1997, but at least he was on. Some of the other guys didn't like it, thought he'd pulled one string too many, got an unfair edge. "Don't worry," he'd tell Wayne. "I'm winning them over. One by one, I'm winning them over."

He'd been riding Engine 3 out of the Grove Street station for two years. He liked the job, probably more than he thought he would. Hadn't seen much fire, though. A couple of house fires his rookie year, one big enough to draw a television cameraman who framed Joe in one of his shots. The guys called him "Hollywood Joe" for a while. Hardly anything burned after that, though, at least not on his shift. But at least he was a fireman now. Contracting was what he did in his spare time, same as plowing the streets after a snowstorm.

He packed up his tools at eleven-thirty and steered his truck out of Charlton. Linda had gone to work that morning, called to the gym to teach an aerobics class for someone else who got sick, but she'd be home by the time Joe got there. Everett and Emily wouldn't be out of school until after two o'clock, which would give them a couple of hours alone. It was a standing date if Joe wasn't working the day shift, just the two of them, rolling around like teenagers.

Linda felt a tingle when she heard Joe's truck in the driveway, then his work boots pounding up the steps. Joe was a big man, six feet tall and 220 pounds. He'd put on weight, forty pounds and almost all of it in his gut since the night she'd met him almost twenty years earlier. If he'd had the belly in 1980, when she was nineteen and he was eighteen, it would have taken him longer to squirrel through the crowd at Tammany Hall, a bar downtown. Linda had gone there with a friend. Joe saw her come through the door, smiled, worked his way over. He called her later that night, two-thirty in the morning, woke up her father. "Please let this be Linda Howe's number," he said. Linda hung up on him, wondering what kind of nut calls a girl at that hour of the morning. She left the phone off the hook so it couldn't ring again until after breakfast, which is when Joe called again. He convinced Linda to go see *The Rose* with him. They saw each other every day after that until they were married in 1986.

After all those years and all those pounds, Linda still thought he was sexy. He had that big Irish mug, bright eyes, and a wide smile. He'd flash it at her across a crowded room and Linda would feel a schoolgirl flush. Then there were the legs. Joe had marvelous legs, lean and strong like a dancer's. If anything, Linda was jealous of them, Joe's skinny thighs.

Joe led her upstairs and into the bedroom. It was Linda's favorite time of the day, the two of them alone in the big pink house Joe had built for her. Minutes melted into hours, the afternoon slipping away, no one minding the time until they heard soft footsteps in the hallway, followed by a light knock on the door.

"Mom? Are you in there?"

Linda and Joe froze. She jerked her head toward the clock. It was after two. Everett was home from school a few minutes early.

"Just a minute," she said. She and Joe got out from under the sheets, fumbled for their clothes, Linda blushing and Joe laughing. "I'll be right out." She stifled a giggle.

"What are you doing in there?"

"I'll be right out," she said again. She dressed quickly, fluffed the mane of chestnut curls that fell below her shoulders, gave Joe a kiss and a playful swat, and opened the door.

Joe smiled to himself, satisfied, happy. *All my dreams came true.* He knew it was a cliché, even thought the phrasing was awkward every time he'd said it out loud to Linda. But it was the truth, especially the last two years. He had a beautiful wife, happy and healthy children, a roof that he'd put over their heads with his own two hands and food on the table he would cook with those same hands. And he was a fireman. An honest-to-God fireman, his father's son.

He realized he was running late, wouldn't have time to stop by his lawyer's office and pick up the check for the two-family house. It was in their old neighborhood, a run-down wreck when he bought it at auction eleven years before. He had fixed it up and rented it out, then fixed it up again after it burned. "It's Everett's college fund," he used to tell Linda. She'd never been crazy about him being a landlord—in fact, she'd never even seen the inside of the building. Now Joe had finally gotten tired of it, too. Dealing with the repairs had become a hassle, so he sold the building. Turned a nice profit, too, doubled his money in a decade. It would have been nice to get his hands on it today, but a few planned hours with Linda were nicer. The check would be there Monday.

He puttered around the house for a while, then got ready for work. He was cooking supper for the guys that night, which meant making two trips out to the car to load the food he'd bought at BJ's Wholesale Club. Just before four-thirty, he told Linda he was leaving and that he'd call to say goodnight to the kids, just like he always did when he had an overnight tour. He said goodbye to Everett, who was in the basement with a friend, and then he called up the stairs. "Emily, I'm leaving."

She didn't answer.

Joe waited a few seconds, pitched his voice up an octave. "'Bye, Daddy, I'll miss you." Down to his normal tone. "I'll miss you, too, Emily. Thanks for the kiss."

"Wait, wait, wait!" He heard her feet padding down the hallway, saw her bound down the stairs. Emily threw her arms around her father's neck, wrapped her legs around his waist, buried her face against his cheek. "'Bye, Daddy," she said. "I'll miss you. I love you."

"I love you, too," Joe said. He kissed her back, kissed his wife again, and went out the door.

Tom Spencer's cell phone trilled above the light hum of afternoon traffic, caught his attention a few blocks out of the grocery store parking lot. "Hello?"

"Hi, it's me. I've got time for lunch. Can you make it?"

Tom brightened. Kathy rarely had time to meet him in the afternoon, especially in the weeks before Christmas. She worked full time managing a medical office, though she only put in a half day on Fridays. Then she scooted out to Paxton, a sleepy town to the northwest, to a nursery where she twisted pine garlands and wrapped poinsettias and tended to the other plants. She went back Saturdays and Sundays, and would through the Christmas rush. They didn't need the money. Tom made a decent living as a lieutenant on Ladder 2, and a few more bucks on the side cleaning office buildings and setting up stages at the Worcester Centrum. That was a good gig. Eighteen dollars an hour for the bull work that kept him in shape, and more for working the lights from the catwalk, which he'd been learning to do the past few nights at the *Holiday on Ice* show. But Kathy liked plants.

"Yeah, of course I can," Tom said. "I'm just coming from the grocery now. I've got stuff for sandwiches, so I'll see you in a few minutes."

Tom did all the grocery shopping and most of the cooking. The finances he left to Kathy. He'd turn over his paychecks, all three of them, and say, "Take care of it." All he wanted was enough money set aside for the family vacations, the trip to the Baseball Hall of Fame in Cooperstown every year, plus a week in France or England or on the rim of the Grand Canyon. Tom had never traveled when he was a boy. By the time he met Kathy, when he was a senior at St. Peter's, Tom had never spent a single night away from home. The first time he'd slept in a different bed was his freshman year at the University of Massachusetts–Lowell, fifty miles to the northeast, but even then he'd come home on weekends, work all night Friday and all day Saturday bagging groceries, go out with Kathy Saturday night, drive back to campus Sunday. He wanted his own three kids to grow up differently, see more of the world.

Kathy found him in the kitchen, layering turkey breast onto whole wheat bread. Tom had been trying to eat healthier the past few years, ever since his cholesterol ticked up. He didn't cut back on the portions, though. Kathy would pack him a lunch when Tom worked the day shift: a sandwich and a piece of fruit. Tom would swallow that by ten o'clock, then have lunch with the rest of the guys at noon. He had a stunning appetite, especially for such a little fellow. "The Lilliputian," some of the guys in the Grove Street station called him. He weighed 150 pounds dripping wet, still wore pants with the same thirty-one-inch waist he had when he took Kathy to see *Jaws* on their first date in 1976. But he was tough. Tom walked up mountains for fun, two thousand vertical feet to the top of Wachusett Mountain once a week or so, his English springer spaniel, Freckles, panting behind him, trying to keep up.

Lunch with Kathy had put him in a particularly good mood.

She would be out of town for the weekend, riding a bus to New York City with their daughter, Casey, and Kathy's best friend, Cheryl. An extra hour with her was a pleasant surprise.

"So what do you want to see in New York?" he asked her.

"I don't know. I've never been there."

Tom nodded, smiled, chewed his sandwich. Tom was a veteran of Manhattan. He made a pilgrimage to see the Metropolitan Opera every year. If he was lucky, he'd catch a performance of *La Bohème,* his favorite. Kathy never went with him because she hated opera, all those CDs Tom had properly alphabetized in a cabinet in the living room. "Tell you what," he said. "I'll make you a walking tour, make sure you see everything. And I'll time it so you can go to mass at St. Patrick's. You can sit for an hour and it won't cost you anything. Try to sit down and have a cup of coffee in New York and you'll have to spend five bucks."

"Would you? That'd be great."

"Yeah, I'll leave a map on the table."

Kathy ate quickly, rushing to make her shift at the nursery. When she finished, Tom walked her to the door, kissed her goodbye. "Oh, hey," he said brightly, "I think tonight's my last night."

"Really?" Kathy had heard that before, a few times during the past month, but Tom always went back to Ladder 2. He was trying to move to the fire-prevention unit, a regular day job inspecting houses and businesses and construction sites. She knew he was torn about it. Tom had been riding a fire truck for twenty years, been the boss—a lieutenant—for seven. He still got juiced by flames, by action. But firemen on the trucks worked a quirky schedule: two-day tours, one day off, two night shifts, three days off, a forty-two-hour week. The prevention job, on the other hand, would be the same four days every week, either Monday through Thursday or Tuesday through Friday. He'd have all his weekends off, more time to spend with three kids who he'd realized lately were growing up much too fast. Patrick, the oldest, was seventeen, a senior in high school; in less than a year he'd be off at college.

Not that he neglected them as it was. Tom was one of those fathers that every man imagines he will be before the rest of his life gets in the way. "The Ozzie Nelson of Grove Street," some of the guys said. When Patrick and Daniel, his youngest, joined the Boy Scouts, so did Tom. He spent lazy summer nights in the backyard, staring up at the sky, teaching his kids how to pick out the constellations, and rainy afternoons in the basement building a miniature town around the HO-scale railroad tracks. If he dragged himself home from an overnight shift and Casey wanted to play tennis, Tom would grab his racket. "Get some rest, you've been working all night," Kathy would tell him. He'd look at her, wide-eyed. "I would never use my job as an excuse not to do something with the kids," he'd say. Working in prevention, he wouldn't have to worry about it.

"Are you sure this time?" Kathy asked.

"That's what they tell me," Tom said. "Tonight's supposed to be my last night. I should be going to prevention on Monday."

Kathy grinned, pecked him on the cheek. "That's great. Enjoy your last night."

4

PAUL BROTHERTON POKED AT THE PHONE, DIALED THE NUMBER for his wife's office. Denise answered on the second ring, which meant she was at her desk at the clinic, Family Health and Social Services. He could picture her sitting there, blond hair drawn back from her face, blue scrubs and white lab coat, both wrinkled by now even though she insisted on ironing every fresh set.

"I'm going in," Paul said. "What time you outta there?"

Denise looked at the clock: ten minutes to five. "Pretty soon. Just gotta put some files away and shut down my computer."

"All right . . ."

"Hey," Denise interrupted. "What's the chance of you booking off tonight?"

A pause. "Why?"

"You can paint the bedroom."

"What are the chances? Absolutely none. I'm not booking off sick to paint a room."

Paul sounded irritated, cranky, which he was. He'd worked an overnight shift on Rescue 1 the night before, got home to Auburn, a bedroom town southwest of Worcester, in the morning, and had been running ever since. He ferried the oldest of their six sons to school at St. John's before driving to his second job, pounding nails for a contractor at a jobsite in Shrewsbury, on the east side of the city. He put in a couple hours of hard labor, then went back to Auburn to pick up Timothy, his nine-year-old, and shuttled him to a doctor's appointment downtown. Now he had to get back to the Central Street station for another over-night tour.

"What's wrong with booking off?" Denise asked. "God, Paul, take a night off. We've got all these people coming over."

"You should've thought about that before you stripped the walls."

"Well, I didn't."

"Too late now. I'm still not calling in sick to paint a bed-room just because you invited a bunch of people over...."

"You know what?" Denise cut him off again. "Go to work. I don't want you home tonight. Just go to work."

Paul let out a small laugh. "I'm going to." Another short pause. "I love you."

"I love you, too. I'll talk to you later."

"Yeah." Paul started to hang up. "Oh, wait. It's pizza night." Friday night was always pizza night—meatless, Catholic pizza night. Saturday night was franks and beans; and Sunday morn-ing, if Paul wasn't working, was breakfast in bed for Denise. "There's a coupon and some money in your jewelry box."

"All right. Thanks."

Paul was only mildly annoyed on the drive into Worcester. Paint a bedroom—what was she, insane? Paul never took a shift off, not unless there was an emergency, like if one of the boys got sick or something. The department was already short-staffed, sending out trucks with too few men to be effective, sometimes too few to even be safe. Christ, he'd been carping about that for years, almost since the day he got on the job in

1983. Denise used to tell him he should go on strike, march around with picket signs until the city hired more men. "Are you nuts?" he'd ask her every time she mentioned it. "I can't go on strike. I'm a fireman, for cryin' out loud. Who's gonna put out the fires?" The last thing Rescue 1 needed tonight, any night, was a goldbricker slopping satin gloss on his bedroom walls.

He wasn't really angry, though. Paul hardly ever got mad at Denise. They hadn't had a real fight since . . . when was it? Four years ago was the last one he could remember, over that stupid corner cabinet in the living room. He still didn't understand why it had to go in a corner. But the bedroom could wait. No one coming over Sunday for Kim's baby shower would be spending much time in there anyway. And Kim wouldn't mind.

She was his little sister, twenty-six now, married. Paul and Denise had raised her from the age of ten, when their parents died, George Brotherton from cancer in May of 1983, Helen from a broken heart two months later. They weren't married yet, Paul and Denise. In fact, Helen died the day after Paul told her he was going to marry Denise. "That's nice," she said. "But I'm afraid I won't be there." She had a massive coronary the next morning, dead before the paramedics got her to Worcester City Hospital. After that, Denise would spend the night when Paul worked an overnight tour, make sure Kim ate dinner and brushed her teeth and went to bed on time. She moved the wedding up, too, so she'd set a better example for Kim.

Paul parked behind the station, in a blacktopped lot surrounded by a rusting chain-link fence. The big overhead doors, four of them that mirrored the four fronting Central Street, were closed against the December chill, so he walked to the corner of the building and gave the pedestrian door a hard tug. It hesitated, then opened with a scrape. Damn door never fit quite right. Paul didn't even notice anymore. After five years living half his life in this station—two days on, two days off, two nights on, three days off—he'd gotten used to the quirks, the loose tiles and peeling paint and wobbly doorknobs. The smell didn't bother him, either, an industrial perfume of fresh diesel and stale smoke. It used to be worse, the diesel stink, before the city finally sprang for the exhaust vacuums, long, flexible tubes that clamped onto the tailpipes of the trucks when they backed into the station after a run. But the smoke stink lingered, always would. Part of it was residue from triple-deckers and tenements, carbonized molecules that had bonded with the gear, fused with the fireproof fibers of the coats hanging on the trucks and in the canvas sheathing of the hoses. The rest of it came from the cigarettes and cigars that no one was supposed to be smoking anyway. Paul wished the bosses would crack down. He'd already quit smoking in the house, in the car, and in front of his boys. If the chief made him light up outside, forced him to stand in the sleet, maybe he'd finally give it up for good. He patted his breast pocket, made sure his Merits were there. Firemen weren't sticklers for a smoke-free workplace.

Paul turned right just inside the door, tromped up a dim stairwell to the second floor, then took a quick right and a quick left down a dingy hallway painted an institutional beige that matched the worn-out linoleum floor. The locker room was halfway down the corridor, set into the middle of the building. The walls in there were brighter. For twenty years, ever since Central Street opened, men had been pasting cheesecake pinups and raunchy centerfolds on the cinderblock. It was a museum of soft-core pornography, faded foldouts of soft-bodied Playmates from the seventies half-covered by siliconed and shaved Pets from the nineties. No one ever complained. All of the firefighters in Worcester were men, and God help the pansy who whined about naked broads on the walls.

In front of his locker, Paul tugged off his jeans, removed his shirt, and hung them on hooks inside. Then he pulled on his work clothes, dark blue trousers and a dark blue sweatshirt with a denim collar and the department shield screened over the heart. He put his badge inside his wallet, and then put his wallet on the shelf inside the locker. Paul never carried his badge on duty. It was sacred, a silver-toned scarab. He would never risk losing it in the frenzy of a fire, dropping it into the ashes. And if his number came up, if God turned to the page where his name was embossed, he didn't want his badge melting in the heat. The dog tags around his neck, the ones the air force gave him when they stranded him in Valdosta, Georgia, for four gnat-infested years, would tell the searchers whose corpse it was.

He had other things in his wallet, important things he didn't want getting burned or soaked. In the center compartment, where the folding money was supposed to go, he had his season ticket for the Massachusetts state lottery. Couldn't lose that—odds were the state would call his number before the good Lord would. And there was a laminated Get Out of Jail Free card from an old Monopoly game, a gag gift that had become a good luck charm of sorts. Couldn't lose that, either.

He also had two pale blue slips of paper, each about the size of a business card, that announced the premiere Worcester performance of the Bobby Watson Band. *"This card good for one free drink!"* each read across the bottom. He'd gotten them when he'd paid the cover at the door of a downtown nightclub called Tammany Hall on June 16, 1983. That was the first night he'd gone out with Denise. It wasn't a date, couldn't have been, since they were both engaged to other people. He'd thought about cashing in the chits at the bar. He tucked them in his wallet instead, paid the bartender cash. He couldn't explain why. Just a feeling.

He double-checked his wallet, made sure it was properly stored in his locker. He started to shut the door, stopped, looked at the photo taped inside. Paul and all six of his boys, lined up on a beach with their backsides to the camera, their trunks pulled down enough to show the tops of their ass cracks. "Beach Bums," he called it. He chuckled to himself again, then swung the door shut. He'd get to the bedroom next week.

The trucks were lined up in their proper bays, four of them, each pointed toward the doors that, when the alarm went off, would open onto Central Street. From the back, which is where most of the men spent most of their time, Engine 1 was on the right, next to the watch room where one man monitored the phone and the radio chatter. Left of the engine was Rescue 1, a boxy van of red enamel and chromed compartments, shorter than any engine or ladder but wide enough to hold five men and all their gear comfortably in the back. Next over was Ladder 1, long as a semitrailer with 110 feet of high-tensile aluminum rungs folded across the back. Against the far wall, near the alcove where the free weights and secondhand Nautilus were set up, was Car 3, a white Ford Expedition with the words "Worcester Fire Department" and "Dial 911" painted on the side. Car 3 was reserved for the north end district chief, which for Paul's shift, Group II, was Mike McNamee.

The entire shift was in the station by five o'clock. Most of them gathered behind Engine 1, where there was a conference table with a wood-grain laminate top, chipped and cracked, and a handful of mismatched chairs, a couple with doubled-over sections of the Worcester *Telegram & Gazette* laid over the springs that stabbed through the upholstery. Secondhand stuff, most of it picked out of the Dumpster behind Commonwealth Stationers. Fraternity house basements had better furnishings.

Paul looked around, took stock of who was on that night. Capt. Robert A. Johnson, a stocky ex-marine with well-creased crow's-feet around his eyes, leaned both elbows on the table, flicking ashes from a generic menthol into a Styrofoam cup that had a splash of cold coffee in the bottom. Three of his regular men—Bob McCann, Jon Davies, Charlie Murphy—were in; the fourth, John King, was on a vacation day, but he'd swapped shifts with another guy to cover for him. His name was Jerry Lucey, a rescue man by trade.

Ladder 1 was all set. Capt. Mike Coakley and his four firefighters were all in, a tight crew of veterans who'd worked together for well more than a decade: his junior man, Bert Davis, had been on the ladder for fourteen years. John Casello, a swarthy fellow who played a mean game of pinochle, and A.C. Davidson, tall with a sandy mustache, were loitering near the kitchen. The fifth ladder man, Steve Connole, was dropping coins in one of the soda machines next to the kitchen. He'd been on Ladder 1 for seventeen years, starting when it was still Aerial Scope 1, an aging truck that was replaced in 1994. "Hey, Yogi, what's up?" Paul said as he passed him. Most people called Connole Yogi, on account of his bearish girth and bottomless gut, which once got him booted out of an all-you-can-eat restaurant before he'd had all that he could, in fact, eat. Yogi grunted back.

On Rescue 1, Lt. Dave Halvorsen, broad-beamed with a military crew cut who looked ten years younger than his early fifties, was missing four of his regular men. Two were on vacation, one was out sick, and another, Gary Williams, had swapped a shift so he could go to a Christmas party with his wife. Craig Boisvert, who normally worked Engine 1 in a different tour group, was filling in for Williams. Halvorsen pulled in another man on overtime, Charlie Rogacz, from a Group III engine. Paul could hear him before he saw him, Charlie's voice like branches grinding through a low-speed wood chipper. Except for Paul and the lieutenant, the only other regular working that night was Tommy Dwyer, a fireplug of a man with white hair and an elaborate mustache that draped like raw wool to his jaw line.

Tommy was Paul's usual partner, the man who crawled next

to him into the boiling black of a fire and sat next to him in the quiet hours at the station, flipping through the television channels until they found Jerry Springer refereeing a white-trash brawl. It was odd, in a way, that Tom and Paul were close, that the two men not only liked each other but routinely placed their lives in each other's hands. Five years earlier, Tom hadn't wanted Paul working Rescue 1. It was nothing personal. Rescue guys, by the nature of their job, were an exceptionally tight bunch. They saw more action than anyone else, for the simple reason that they were dispatched to every working fire in the city. An engine in one of the quieter neighborhoods might go six weeks without catching a whiff of smoke. And on the fire ground, rescue work seemed more dangerous, or at least more daring. Engine companies extinguished the fire, actually put the wet stuff on the red stuff. Ladder guys opened the building—bashed doors, smashed windows, chopped holes in the roof—to let the engine men in and to let the smoke and the heat out. While that was going on, the rescue men plunged inside, searching for flames that might have spread or people who might be trapped. They carried only rudimentary tools—a flathead ax or a medieval-looking truncheon called a Haligan—but never a hose that could beat back a sudden blowup or wash a retreat through a fast-sprouting forest of orange. Their job wasn't necessarily more important and wasn't even always more perilous. But if fighting fire was a war, and some nights it was, the rescue men would be walking point.

That's where Paul had always wanted to be, on point. He'd logged eleven years on engines and ladders, learning the rudiments, all the basic skills required to control and conquer fire. Partly, he figured he'd need to know all that to be a good rescue man. Mostly, he needed a decade under his belt before he had enough seniority to force his way onto the truck. That finally happened in 1994. There was one open slot on Rescue 1, which for a few months had been temporarily filled by a fireman named Jimmy. He expected to get the official appointment, become a permanent rescue man, and was so sure of it he had the Rescue 1 shield bolted to his helmet. He was good at the job, and the other men liked him. They wanted to keep him on the team.

Then Paul asked to be transferred. Tom Dwyer called him at home, tried to discourage him. "Look, I'm not telling you what to do," he said. "I mean, it's your right. You've got the seniority. But I'm just saying, the guys like Jimmy. Nobody wants to see him go."

"Too bad," Paul said. "I've waited ten years for this. I want it."

"Hey, you do what you want. I'm just telling you, the guys like Jimmy. A lot."

"Tough."

Jimmy was sent to an engine. Paul transferred in, got a chilly reception. He started hearing whispers through the department grapevine, secondhand grumblings, nothing directly to his face. *You never know what can happen in a fire. Guys can get lost, get left behind. All kinds of things can happen.* Station house grousing. All bluffs, too, because no man worth his badge would leave a brother in trouble. The whole point of being a fireman is to save people. But Paul was rattled enough to mention it to his chief, Mike. "Let it go," Mike told him. "They'll get over it. You'll be fine."

Which he was. It didn't take long, either. It was hard not to like Paul. He was a chronic smart-ass, an ever-flowing fountain of wisecracks. Even in the shower, standing buck naked, he'd pop off. He eyeballed a bald guy once, staring at his scalp, then at his furry back, then up to the head, down to the black-haired shoulders. "Jesus," he said, as if he'd discovered an enormous bug under a rock. "God sure has a weird sense of humor, huh?" In the station house, being funny, even viciously so, was a survival skill. So was being able to take it. The patter was a cacophony of taunts and put-downs, vicious verbal jabs and savage parries, the sharp squish of balls getting busted. And that was among guys who *liked* each other. The outcasts, the handful of men marked as cowards or cretins or ass-kissers, were either mercilessly harassed or completely ignored. It was hard to tell which was worse: a firehouse is a miserable place if no one likes you, and an awfully lonely place if no one will talk to you. But everyone talked to Paul. Everyone liked Paul.

5

MIKE MCNAMEE CROSSED THE APPARATUS FLOOR A FEW MIN-utes before five-thirty, coming from the far side, where Car 3 was parked, toward the kitchen. He saw Paul Brotherton heading his way, stocky legs taking deliberate strides, solid arms swinging from wide shoulders. He heard Paul say something—not the words, only the tone. A wisecrack. Had to be, because it always was.

Mike let out a low laugh on cue, shook his head, grinned. Didn't matter what the joke was. It was probably harmless and probably funny. "Evenin', Paul," he said.

"Chief." Paul kept walking, disappeared around the far side of Rescue 1.

Mike was distracted, his mind wandering, thinking about his father. Dead two years today, almost to the hour. The last time Mike saw him was a Monday night, December 1, 1997, the night William V. McNamee started driving south to Florida. Mike gave him a bear hug, stepped back, poked him gently in the chest. "If you get tired, you pull over," Mike told his father. Mock stern. "Got it?"

His father nodded patiently, the way men do when they're

being lectured by the children they've raised. But he kept his word. Two days later, just after six o'clock in the evening, he turned off the interstate in Maryland, looking for a hotel he used to stay in with his wife before she died. He made a couple of wrong turns, took his eye off the road, and drove into the back end of a tractor trailer. He died instantly.

Mike had to tell two of his three sisters. Hardest calls he'd ever made, his fingers trembling when he dialed, his voice weak, cracking when he said the words. He tried not to dwell on it, usually didn't. But the anniversary was tough.

He passed behind Engine 1 and veered sharply to the right, aiming for the coffeepot. At the table, sitting on the mismatched chairs, he saw Jerry Lucey and Craig Boisvert. He knew them well enough to recognize their faces, remember their names. Craig was fairly new, only a couple years on the job, and assigned to a different tour group. Promising kid. Jerry was more famil- iar. He worked on the HazMat team with Mike, but unless a tanker flipped on I-290 or a chlorine tank sprung a leak, he didn't see him much. Mike knew his reputation, though. Driven, aggressive, one of those guys who was born with soot in his blood, a fireman long before he ever took the test or drove an engine or climbed a ladder. Jerry wanted the job so bad that he quit driving a truck for Coca-Cola and took a seat among the doomed recruits of 1991; the city had already announced layoffs for the following year. Last in, first out, which meant Jerry and the rest of the recruits would be laid off as soon as they finished their training. He stuck it out for a year, supporting his wife and two boys with odd jobs, until he was recalled in July 1992. Nine months later, he was riding Rescue 1. A rookie working rescue was unheard of, but Jerry wanted it so bad, drove so hard, the captain took him on anyway. Now a seven-year veteran, he taught at the Massachusetts Firefighting Academy, marched in the color guard.

"A fireman's fireman," the other guys said about Jerry. "A *good* fireman," the highest compliment anyone could ever hear in the station. Oh, there might be slightly more effusive praise. If, say, a man snatched a baby from a melting crib, he might have been told "Good save." But only in a gruff mumble. Firemen were low-key with praise, reflexively averse to fawning, which was fine since most of them tended toward humility, almost as if they feared taunting the fire gods with any giddy display of bravado. Better to do the job quietly, professionally.

"Hello, gentlemen," Mike said as he passed. "So, who are you two supposed to be tonight?"

"I swapped on for John King," Jerry said.

"And I'm in for Gary Williams," Craig said.

Mike nodded, pulled a Styrofoam cup from the stack, lifted the black lever on the silver pot.

"Uh, Chief?"

Mike looked over his shoulder. Jerry was talking. Except for his slightly elfin ears, he bore a striking resemblance to Tom Hanks, or what Hanks would look like after the wardrobe and makeup people got him ready to walk onto a firehouse set: dark Celtic eyes and jet-black hair, a thick, almost Victorian, mustache.

"Would you mind if we worked our own trucks?"

Mike stared at them blankly. He aligned their faces with their trucks, Jerry on the rescue, Craig on the engine. "Why would we want to do that?" he deadpanned. "That makes sense." He waited for a laugh, or at least a chuckle. Jerry and Craig looked at him, as though they weren't sure if the chief was serious. "Yeah, of course," Mike said. "Go ahead."

He finished filling his cup from the pot, then started walking back across the floor. He did a quick head count. Only one truck was running short out of Central tonight. Not bad. Better than a lot of other nights, truth be told. It used to be much worse, the short-staffing. Back in the eighties, after the budget got so badly squeezed, more than half the trucks were going out with only three men on them, the equivalent of fielding a football team without an offensive line. Guys were doing solo rescues, stumbling into black passages alone, no one to back them up, bail them out if things went bad. There was one night a lady jumped from a flaming fifth-floor window because the ladder truck didn't have enough men to raise the fifty-five footer in time. They had to recruit a civilian—a freaking civilian—to hoist it up. They missed Constance Walker by fifteen seconds. When she jumped, she bounced off the ladder man climbing up to get her. She died when she hit the pavement.

Mike had good men working tonight, too. A cohesive group, almost all veterans. Mike went back years with most of those guys, decades, some of them. Johnny Casello, as competent a ladder man as the city had ever seen, had been in his drill class in 1972. The officers—Halvorsen, Coakley, Johnson—were three of the best in the department. Smart, seasoned, aggressive. He was especially close to Coakley, a relative by marriage, Joanne's cousin. "No family trees in Worcester," Mike used to muse. "Just one big, tangled wreath." Plus, he'd taught with Coakley in the eighties, when they were both assigned to the drill school. Paul Brotherton had been in their first class. So had Yogi. Three more men working out of Central that night—Bert Davis on the ladder, Bobby McCann on the engine, Tommy Dwyer on the rescue—had been Mike's students. Good firemen, Mike told himself, every one of them.

Teaching had been his idea, a request he'd made after ten years on the street. He'd had a good run, moved up fast. After two years on Ladder 7 out of Winslow Street, a crumbling, rat-infested shack of a station, he got onto Rescue 1. Five years later, he was promoted to lieutenant and sent to run his own truck, Engine 4 in the Park Avenue station, just north of downtown. A good district, fiery enough to keep a man busy, give him a regular fix. But he was still an egghead, worked a lot of the job in his head. He digested dense monographs and trade journals, kept current with advances in equipment and techniques, all of which made him a bit of an oddity. Firemen were creatures of habit, products of their own experience; they weren't much for newfangled gimmicks and book-read theories. Firefighting was a job learned by doing, by charging into the flames with a hose and an ax and a gut full of courage. And once a man conquered a fire, once he'd stood in the center of a furnace and walked back out, once mortal combat became a matter of routine, he was reluctant to change his methods.

Generations of firefighters, for instance, had worn the same basic battle gear—rubber waders that rose to the middle of the thigh and a long, heavy coat that fell just below the top of the boots. Standing straight and still, a man was fully protected; wrench too hard to one side or reach up too high and the coat shifted, exposed the lip of the boot, which would pucker into a funnel and catch water or, worse, a hot ember. By the late 1970s, however, lightweight, heat-resistant fibers had made full trousers practical. But hardly anyone wore them. A curious logic was invented to justify it, too: fireproof pants—quick hitches, in the jargon, or bunker pants—prevented men from feeling heat on their thighs, which gave them a false sense of security and thus made their job *more* dangerous, not less. Mike had heard that argument. Then he heard Bobby Woods got caught in a backdraft that blew his coat up around his waist. He visited Bobby in the hospital, saw the black scars charred into his groin and belly. Mike bought a pair of quick hitches after that, the first man in Worcester to routinely wear them.

Controlling his own equipment was no problem. But Mike saw other things, nagging inefficiencies that required a more systemic redress. Like the way hoses were fed. Worcester had strong

water mains—tap a hydrant and the liquid spewed out like an
uncorked geyser, a torrent more than adequate to feed two of the
department's biggest hoses simultaneously. So Worcester firemen
routinely attached their attack lines—the hoses that sprayed water on the flames—directly to the hydrants. In the days of horse-
drawn hose wagons and, later, primitive pumper trucks, the
vigorous supply was a blessing, allowing the men to put a maxi-
mum of wet stuff on the red stuff. It became a habit: the first engine on the scene would screw a Y-shaped valve onto the hydrant
and run a pair of lines off it, the second engine would go find another hydrant, and so on, until hundreds of yards of hose had
been dragged across rough asphalt and sharp curbs, stout cables
crisscrossing the street like so many unraveled threads.

There was no need for such a tangle. Each of the department's engines were outfitted with pumps that could feed five,
and sometimes six, hoses at once, all from a single connection
to one hydrant. And the pumps could regulate the water pressure more efficiently; connecting a line directly to the main
required wrenching back the hydrant to slow the flow, an im-
precise and laborious method. Mike explained that to the
brass, suggested that their engines were being used as over-
priced hose wagons.

"What's the matter with the way we been doin' it?" the older
guys would snap. "You saying we're doin' it wrong?"

"No, no, no," Mike would answer. "I'm just saying that
there's a better way to—"

"A better way? So we're doin' it wrong. That's what you're
saying, right? We've been doing it wrong?"

That was when Mike decided to teach, work with the young
guys before they could fall into the old routines, shake things
up. He stayed with it for five years, long enough to get more
than 120 recruits onto the trucks. About a quarter of them were
assigned to Group II, five to his home station. He was responsi-

ble for what they learned years ago. Now he was responsible for getting them home at the end of the shift.

The alarm squawked from the speaker bolted to the wall at about quarter past five. Every man froze. Their muscles tensed. Their adrenal glands quivered. No one made a sound, waiting for the next noise out of the speaker. Most times, only words followed. "Engine 1," dispatch might have said, or "Engine 8," or "Ladder 5"—but only one truck—before reciting an address and a task. One tone signaled a medical run or some other minor emergency, like going out to stabilize a coronary case until an ambulance arrived, or breaking a toddler out of a locked-up Taurus, or squirting water on a flaming car. Milk runs.

Sometimes, maybe every fifth time, a second tone followed the first. Two tones meant something more serious, perhaps a fire alarm ringing somewhere, but probably triggered by nothing more than a stray wisp of cigarette smoke or a burp of electrical current jiggling a circuit. Dispatch sent two engines and one ladder truck for those, picking whichever units were available and close.

Much rarer were three tones. Three tones meant a reported structure fire, a house or a condo or a strip mall already blowing smoke into the sky. Firemen longed for a triple. Three tones meant there would be blazing orange heat and churning black clouds and pockets of poison gas, wailing sirens and blinding lights and scalding steam and great, splashing floods. Three tones meant bashing in steel doors and smashing out glass windows and chopping jagged holes through steep, pitched roofs. Men with long metal spears and iron hooks would rip into ceilings and walls, chasing veins of fire hiding behind the plaster and above the joists. Yards of hose would uncoil through puddles of sooty water, and ladders would stretch up a hundred teetering feet. The sensations, the sights and sounds and smells, would be horrifying and exhilarating all at once. "Enough fire for everyone," is what the veterans would say if the fire really started raging, and they would say it giddily, greedily, like little boys who'd stumbled into an unlocked candy shop.

Three tones didn't always turn out that way, of course, and not every man wished that they would. (One of the theorems of the station house was the Rule of Three, which held that every fire required three times more men to show up than were needed to put it out because one third wouldn't want to be there and another third wouldn't know what they were doing.) But a working fire promised at least the chance of action, and that is what a certain breed of firefighter craved. Paul, Jerry, Yogi, Robert A., Captain Coakley, nearly every man on Central Street was of that breed. They would feel more alive when confronted by the possibility of death, surrounded by it, threatened by it. They would not be afraid but only aware, in the same way that an alpinist, cramponed to a rock high above a thin and frigid void, was aware of gravity. The challenge was neither reckless nor foolhardy—indeed, because the danger was so obvious and omnipresent firefighters were exceedingly conscious of any signals that preceded a life-threatening shift in conditions—but it was enthralling. Every nerve tingled, a tremble that started in the primitive stem of the brain and skittered, like electricity through bare copper wire, into the arms, the legs, the chest, the gut.

So the men tensed at the first honk from the wall. Then they relaxed at the bored voice, all that excitable juice soaking back into their tissues. "Engine 3," the dispatcher began.

Not one of their trucks. Engine 3 ran out of the Grove Street station. No one in Central had to move at all. That's when they stopped listening completely.

6

JAY LYONS JOGGED ACROSS THE CEMENT FLOOR OF THE GROVE Street station as the dispatcher repeated the order for Engine 3 to roll, moving quickly but not with any enthusiasm. He hauled himself behind the wheel, switched on the motor, goosed the gas pedal, forced a growl out of the big diesel. Three more men, bulky in their bunker pants and turnout coats, piled into the compartment behind the cab. Jay's boss, Lt. John Sullivan, climbed into the passenger seat. The overhead door facing Grove Street rolled up and back, opening a portal into the December dusk. "Let's go," Sullivan said. Jay dropped the transmission into gear and stepped harder on the gas. Sully yanked the cord for the air horn, toggled the siren, sent the engine onto the street with a yowl and a wail.

The first run of the night, a medical assist. Jay had long ago gotten tired of one-bell runs. Most engine men eventually did. There were just so damned many of them, sixteen thousand a year, give or take, more than half of any engine company's workload. It was a good theory, sending a truck out to every medical emergency dialed into 911. Every Worcester fireman was trained in advanced first aid, and with fifteen engines operating out of a dozen stations in every corner of the city, they usually beat the ambulances to the scene. There were some good calls, too, ones that made the guys feel like they were doing something important, actually helping someone. Every couple of months, an engine crew would help a woman through her last moments of labor, bring a new life into the world, or restart a heart with the defibrillator, keep an old life hanging on a little longer.

But most first-responder runs didn't amount to much more than baby-sitting until the ambulance showed up. Like this one, chugging to a gym on Millbrook Street where a diabetic had passed out while lifting weights. The men from Engine 3 would keep him warm, monitor his vital signs, wait for the paramedics to take over. A useful task. There were worse calls to get. People dialed 911 for ridiculous reasons: an upscale private club used the firemen and the ambulance drivers to bounce its drunks, insisting their stumbling belligerence was merely a gentleman's seizure. Sunburns and menstrual cramps became emergencies after midnight. One of the engine companies was on a first-name basis with a petite homosexual hustler who called every few months complaining about his bleeding rectum.

It wasn't the kind of action Jay had signed up for. Jay lusted for fire, monstrous, voracious flames, untamable incinerators, the infernos that hardly ever reared up in Worcester anymore. He'd been through a couple, even taped a picture inside his locker to remind himself it could happen again. It was black-and-white, reprinted from a newspaper, a three-family tenement disintegrating in flames two years earlier. Jay wrote in the margin, "My first big blaze!" He tolerated the first-responders the way an athlete tolerates wind sprints: required drudgery for a chance to play in the big game.

At least it was his night to drive. Jay mashed the pedal to the floor, flattening it with his boot, accelerating north on Grove. Cars on the road slowed, moved to the curb, parting before the shriek and roar of the engine. Jay backed off the gas at the corner of Glennie Street, pulled the wheel around to the right, hand over hand, leaning into the turn. The best part of a bad run, sitting high and forward, a captain on a flat sea of blacktop. "When I'm driving Engine 3," he'd tell his father every so often, "I'm living every little boy's fantasy." Which he knew was true because it had been his fantasy.

Jay had been hanging around firehouses since he was old enough to pedal his bike to the Park Avenue station, a few blocks from the house where he grew up. When he was a little older, he'd be at headquarters twice a month with Explorer Post 201 listening to one of the veterans talk about the finer and more gruesome aspects of the job—how to lay a hose or smother a chemical fire or cut an unconscious passenger out of a mangled Buick. He clipped stories of spectacular fires from the newspaper, pasted them into scrapbooks, read them, studied them, imagined himself in an oversize coat and a heavy helmet, rushing into the flames and carrying out a body, limp and barely alive. At night, he'd lie in bed listening to the chatter on a Bearcat 210XL eighteen-channel scanner, waiting for the three telltale tones. Then he'd jostle his father awake. "C'mon, dad," he'd jabber. "We're going to a fire." If the flames were close enough, if the hour was early enough, Jim Lyons always took his boy. If the fire was stubborn, if it took the men longer to wash it away than Jim felt like waiting, he would sometimes leave his son. He knew Mike McNamee would get him home.

Mike lived across the street in a yellow Cape on Saxon Road, a winding semicircle in a leafy neighborhood west of downtown. Jay was twelve when Mike and Joanne moved in with their two daughters. A real smoke-eater, living right outside his bedroom window. And on Rescue 1! Those guys went to all the fires, got to do the coolest work. Mike would tell Jay about the big fires, the worst fires, the scariest fires, feed his imagination.

Some nights, if Jay didn't have school the next morning, Mike would find him a spare bunk at Central Street, let him spend the night like a real fireman.

It seemed to be hardwired into him, Jay's fascination with fighting fires. No one in his family, four generations of Worcester stock, had ever worked for the department, except for the time his great-grandfather took a spot on a bucket brigade. But Jay was enthralled with the tradition, the gallantry. It was a romantic image, one seared into his mind by the heat of a fire one cold winter morning. Three sharp brays from the Bearcat woke him up. The fire was close, only five houses away. Jay scrambled out of bed, pulled on some clothes, and sprinted down the sidewalk. The flames had begun with a loose electrical wire, a spark that burrowed into the wall, fed on insulation and studs, then broke through, grabbing curtains and furniture and wood moldings. When Jay got there, the whole house was burning bright, wrapped in fire and bellowing smoke. The first engines were at the curb, men dragging the line to a hydrant, wrenching the coupling into place.

One of Jay's neighbors stood barefoot in the street, screaming. "There's someone inside! The old guy's still inside!"

Three firefighters forced open the front door, crawled to the kitchen, all the way in the back. They felt a body on the floor near the door, an elderly man choked unconscious. The firemen hauled him out the back and started working on him, pumping his chest and breathing hard into his mouth. It was too late. The old man died at City Hospital less than an hour later.

But they'd tried to save him. That's what Jay remembered, the important part. Years later, in the winter of 1983, Jay wrote an essay for his application to Clark University. In cramped and slanted cursive, he wrote about Explorer Post 201, and then told the whole story of the fire—"a significant experience or achievement that has special meaning for you," according to the instructions on the essay sheet—from the moment he woke up until the old man died at the hospital.

"'Fools rush in where angels fear to tread' is a quote that many people would use to describe firefighters," he wrote at the end of his essay.

> Seeing these men rush into this house made me wonder why they do this. Why did these men risk their lives for someone they didn't even know? The answer is not found in the quote, because these men are not fools, and the answer is not because they are being paid for it. The answer itself is very simple, this is their life, the life of saving others.

Sixteen years later, on a night just as cold as that winter morning, he was behind the wheel of a Worcester Fire Department engine. He wasn't saving anyone. He was going to hold the hand of a passed-out diabetic, play nursemaid for some guy who forgot to snarf down a candy bar. That was his life, another goddamned medical assist.

Engine 3 rolled through the gloaming, the road ahead strobing red and white, puddles of light swirling across the blacktop and the sidewalks and the storefronts. Jay liked the view from the cab better after dark, the flashes and reflections, the streaky contrast of sharp colors against the muted gray of night. He stopped complaining about the task at hand, even if it had been only to himself. He was lucky to be back on a fire truck, living his little-boy dream. A second chance at a fantasy—how many guys got that?

He couldn't remember exactly how he'd screwed everything up. He could piece the main narrative together from what he'd read in the newspapers and what the prosecutor argued at his trial and what the other cops said before they kicked him off the force. But the details were lost, washed away in a flood of foamy beer.

It had happened four years ago, on a night like this, when the sky was cold and gray and autumn was losing ground to winter. He was sitting behind the wheel of his car, drunk, staring at the black pool of the Atlantic splashing out to the horizon, spilling into the abyss beyond the curve of the earth. He fiddled with a .38 revolver in his lap. His personal sidearm, not the one the Massachusetts State Police had given him along with a badge three years before.

He'd left the Worcester Fire Department in 1992. After more than four years of riding Engine 1, Jay was restless, tired of waiting for alarms that hardly ever rang. The frantic chatter he'd heard on his Bearcat—two, three, four fires a night—had been replaced by single tones and long hours of silence. He looked into his own future, saw three decades drag out, him sitting in a worn-out chair around a chipped table, his belly starting to fold over his belt, muscles melting, crazy with boredom, waiting for something to burn. So when the state police offered him a job, he took it. Maybe policing would have more action. Maybe he'd catch a killer or a rapist or a bank robber. If nothing else, he'd be in a cruiser, moving, accelerating. His mother warned him not to go. "Stay with the fire department," she'd told him. "It's what you've always wanted to do." He should've listened to her.

The strange thing was, he liked being a cop. At first, anyway. He patrolled the two-lane roads and drowsy hamlets near the Vermont border for eighteen months, then was rewarded with a transfer to Martha's Vineyard. He thought he'd be happy there, out in the middle of the ocean, surrounded by sea breezes that smelled like the beach at Green Harbor, smelled like all those boyhood summers in his parents' cottage. During the warmer months, tourists swarmed the island, pretty girls with money and suntans, a smorgasbord for a handsome young man in a well-pressed uniform.

Then came Labor Day. The whole place cleared out, eighty-five thousand summer folk leaving all at once. Only the fishermen and the tradesmen and the drunkards stayed behind. Shops and restaurants shuttered. August mistrals gave way to February gales raking the desolate rock. There wasn't much for anyone to do, and less for a cop: the crimes were minor, and the miscreants were back on the same streets two days later, eyeballing the pig who'd handcuffed them.

Jay suffered through one winter, put in another summer tour, then asked to be shipped back to the mainland. In early November 1995, his request was denied. That's how he ended up staring at the water, fiddling with a gun. He'd started drinking at four o'clock that afternoon. It only got him more worked up. By ten o'clock—this was where the details got fuzzy—he was hammered and ranting, complaining about drug dealers, how the island had to be cleaned up and the bad guys taught a lesson. He got in his car and drove to Oak Bluffs, one of the villages on the Vineyard. Downtown was a big gray house where a drug dealer lived, a bad guy with a record going back to the Nixon administration. Jay himself had arrested the guy a few months earlier with a hundred bags of heroin. Now he was out on bail, loosed on the same claustrophobic island.

Jay stuck his arm out the window of his car, pointed the pistol at the house. He squeezed the trigger, once, twice, two quick shots through the clapboards. One lodged in the couch, the other in a bookcase. Then Jay squealed into the night, thirsty, back to a barroom. An hour later, he returned to Oak Bluffs, joyriding in front of the Strand Theater, firing a half-dozen more rounds into the air.

He was arrested, of course. The state police fired him, a jury eventually convicted him, a judge gave him two years in jail, all but ninety days suspended. With time off for good behavior, Jay left the Dukes County House of Correction in February 1997. He hadn't taken a drink in more than two years by then, ever since that night with the gun. But he was still an ex-con and a disgraced cop. He found work driving a school bus, manning the door at a nightclub, substitute teaching. Odd jobs, nothing steady. He wished he'd never left the fire department.

Mike McNamee finally asked him about coming back. Mike had been one of the only people who thought Jay should be a cop, at least try it. "Look at it this way," he'd told him back in 1992. "If you don't do it, you're always gonna wonder. You're always going to think, *what if?* What if I'd been a cop instead of a fireman? Take a leave of absence. You can take, what, five years? If you don't like it you can always come back. What've you got to lose?"

Five years later, Jay thought he knew the answer to that question: almost everything. Now Mike was offering a shot at redemption. They were standing at the foot of Mike's driveway, a warm spring day in 1997, nubby red buds on the hydrangeas, baby leaves on the maples scattering the sunlight. Jay was sweaty from a run. He heard Mike ask him, "When's your five years up?"

Jay gave him a curious look. "My five years? What do you mean?"

"You took a five-year leave of absence, right? When's it up?"

Jay did the math in his head. "Um, August. Why?"

"What about coming back? I mean, to the department. You ever think about it?"

He'd never stopped thinking about it. When he was a cop, he still kept his gear by the front door, his boots lined up just so in the foyer, his turnout coat hanging on peg. "Yeah, of course," Jay answered. "But, you know, I can't."

"Actually, I think you might be able to."

Jay snapped his head around, bore his eyes into Mike's.

"I don't want to get your hopes up," Mike said. "But I think you can still go back. I don't think there's anything on the books that says you can't, even with a record. I know there's a thing in there about felonies, but . . ." He paused, unsure of the legal technicalities. "Look," he said, "why don't you start researching the law."

Jay dug through the civil service rules, found the page with the right loophole. He hadn't spent enough time in jail to disqualify himself. Mike, meanwhile, went to see the chief, Dennis Budd, to put in a good word for Jay. It wasn't hard. Budd had always liked Jay, thought he'd been a good fireman the first time around. In July, Budd agreed to give Jay a job. Jay told him, "You won't be disappointed, Chief. I won't let you down, I promise."

The diabetic survived. The ambulance arrived just after Engine 3, packed him up, took him to the hospital. Jay trudged back to the truck, Lieutenant Sullivan a few steps behind him. The other three men—Joe McGuirk, Mark Fleming, Doug Armey—climbed into the back. Jay kicked the engine over and started the slow drive back to Grove Street. They'd be back to the station by quarter to six, plenty of time before dinner.

A few blocks away from the gym, Sully shifted in his seat, pushed his shoulders back, gave the air an exaggerated sniff. "Gonna be a big one tonight," he said. He was smiling. "I can smell it."

Jay gave him a sideways glance. Sully said that almost every night, and he was wrong every time. Jay had been back on the job for more than two years, but Engine 3 still hadn't seen a fire that a good squirt from a two-and-a-half couldn't handle. The other three guys on the truck, Mark, Doug, and Joe, had never been in a real burner. They were all fairly new, only a couple of years out of drill school even though Joe, at thirty-eight, was the oldest man on the truck. The three rookies were part of the reason Jay had been assigned to Engine 3. He was only thirty-four, but a grizzled veteran compared to everyone but Sully. If Jay hadn't left for five years, he was sure he'd be running his own truck by now. As it was, he was on the promotions list for lieutenant, having taken the test after rejoining the fire department. He was just waiting for a slot to open up. Early next year, he figured, maybe February. In the meantime, putting Sully and Jay on the same engine made sense, two qualified men to supervise three rookies. If things got hairy, Sully knew he could count on Jay to help look after everyone.

They'd come on the job together, Sully and Jay, in 1987. In some ways, they were strikingly similar: both were aggressively intelligent, almost cocky, eager to prove how smart they were. They were the top two graduates in their drill class, Jay a fraction of a point ahead. And part of the reason he took the test for the state police, not to mention the New York City Fire Department exam, was just to see how well he'd score. Sully started studying for a promotion almost as soon as he learned to drive the trucks; he made lieutenant after only six years, when he was thirty-one. Six years later, he was next in line to make captain.

Yet they were very different firefighters. Sully was a book man, methodical, controlled. If Engine 3 was second due—that is, if it was slotted to be the second engine on the scene, which meant it was supposed to tap a hydrant to supply the first-due guys lugging lines into the fire—he was going to be second in, even if it meant letting a slower truck overtake him. It was neither glamorous nor exciting, but it had to be done, and Sully believed in doing the job properly. Most of the department's procedures were outlined in manuals, handbooks, and memos, most of which Sully knew by heart and followed to the letter. It made him a good instructor, always lecturing at some academy or seminar.

Jay used to tease him about that. "Those who can't do," he'd say, "teach." It came out as a joke, but there was an undercurrent of a sneer. Jay thrived on chaos, action. "Ballsy," Sully called him, always wanting to jump into the hottest, smokiest patch of hell he could find. If the first-due truck couldn't keep up, fuck 'em. Let those guys grab the hydrant, let Jay rush the flames. If he was driving Engine 3, Sully would be sitting next to him flipping through a thick pamphlet that listed the location of every hydrant and specifying which ones should be tapped for which addresses. "Will you get your head out of that fucking book," Jay would yell at him. "Let's just grab a fucking hydrant and move." Good fires were hard to come by in Worcester, and Jay didn't want to miss any chance to storm into the flames.

"Yep," Sully said again. "Big one coming." He drew in another breath, his heavy black mustache curling beneath his nostrils, air filling his lungs, puffing out his chest. "Three alarms. You smell it? I smell it."

Jay snorted, shook his head. "Yeah, three alarms. And it'll be on the south side and we won't be going."

He turned Engine 3 onto the apron in front of the station, steered it into a loping turn, angling the rear toward the third door from the left. Joe, Doug, and Mark hopped down from the back, flanked the truck near the back bumper, and guided Jay into the garage. The door rolled closed. Jay cut the motor and climbed down from the cab.

7

THE MATCH SPARKED AND BLOSSOMED INTO A FLAME. JULIE held it between her thumb and first two fingers, the nails chewed off and the tips raw, and touched the droplet of fire to a Christmas candle on the crate next to the bed. The wick caught, and an orange flower of light sprouted from a red wax stem. The darkness receded, but only a few feet; the edges of the room blurred into indistinct shadows.

It wasn't very big, the room, about the size of a county jail cell or a small clerk's office, which is what it had been before the warehouse closed down a decade before. The clutter made it seem more cramped, but it was still better than the shelters. The bed was in the middle: a wooden pallet layered with blankets, two spread across the slats as a mattress, five more on top for warmth. To the right of the bed, near the foot of the pallet, was a kerosene heater that fought back the chill on the coldest nights. Most of the clothes, filthy sweatshirts and worn jeans, were piled against the left wall, but a few tattered garments were scattered around the room, jumbled with the trash, scraps of half-eaten food, cellophane wrappers, paper bags. Opposite the bed was a tiny closet, on the floor of which was a box overflow-

ing with cat feces. The human waste was deposited outside the
sleeping quarters, in the hallways and downstairs near the door
that opened onto the loading dock of Worcester Cold Storage.
The place smelled like a sewer. Julie had gotten used to it.

She didn't live there anymore, not since she'd broken up
with Tom. This was his place. He'd jimmied one of the doors
last spring. Tom was good at that, finding places to squat. When
he was with Celine, he broke them into a rusty trailer in a vacant lot at the foot of Grafton Street, on the edge of the old
warehouse district. After she got sent to prison for drugs, he
found his way into Worcester Cold Storage. It was supposed to
be locked, sealed like a tomb, the few windows sheathed in plywood, the doors padlocked. But Tom could figure a way inside
almost anything. He'd had a lot of practice, nineteen years of it,
almost half his whole life living on the streets. Besides, no one
seemed to care that he was living in there. Right after Halloween, a cop searched the building with his police dog. Part of
it, anyway; the cop, gagging on the stench, left after a few minutes because he was afraid his dog would get sick.

It was perpetually dark inside, so Tom kept a flashlight hidden behind a steel beam on the loading dock. He would follow
a spot of light through the maze of meatlockers and corridors,
sidestepping the rubbish and muck, up to the office on the second floor, where he'd arranged the furniture. Other than the
filth, though, the warehouse was good shelter. Sturdy, much
more solid than the trailer, or most any other building for that
matter. The brick walls were eighteen inches thick, and the
floors were held up with timber joists the size of tree trunks
that rested on columns of lumber and cast iron spaced every
twelve feet. Because it had been used for cold storage, the walls
were layered with insulation striated like bedrock: sheets of
cork cemented together with asphalt, which were then covered
with polyurethane and polystyrene as the years passed, and, in

spots where the surface had to be smooth, a thin laminate. It wasn't exactly warm inside, but the walls held in the heat from the kerosene and kept out the worst arctic cold. A nor'easter could blow the city apart and Tom, huddled under his dirty blankets, likely wouldn't even hear it.

Julie had lived there with him, off and on, throughout the summer and most of the fall. Tom had gotten her pregnant right on this bed, sometime around Labor Day. But she didn't want to be his girlfriend anymore. Tom was jealous, which was perhaps understandable because Julie would hook up with other guys for a few weeks at a time, like that guy Scott she met in September at the day-labor pool. Tom had a temper, too. Sometimes, when he got mad, he would get rough with her, not beat her up or anything but push her around enough to make her miserable. He had a reputation for hitting women. A couple of old girlfriends had even gotten restraining orders against him. Julie left him— again—around Thanksgiving. She'd spent the first nights of December in a cheap hotel room with a fellow named Bruce, but her stuff was still in the warehouse. A lot of her clothes, her coloring book, her crayons. And her animals. Julie loved animals. She had a cat, a black short-hair, and a mongrel dog. The dog was sick, which is why she came back, to check on him.

She heard shuffling footsteps in the hallway. Tom. Julie had expected he would show up. She'd seen him outside, in the gloom near the Kenmore Diner, watching her as she ambled up Franklin Street and around the corner of Arctic toward the dock in the back. She knew he would follow her.

"What are you doin' here?"

Tom stood just inside the room. The glow from the candle put his face into relief, made his cheeks more hollow, his eyes more sunken. His shadow, pale in the dusky light, was a slender thread slinking across the floor and partway up one wall.

"I'm checking on my dog," Julie said. She sounded pouty, like a young child, which, fundamentally, she was. She was nineteen years old, and she had enough street savvy to survive—where to go for a free meal or, if she didn't have a boyfriend who would put her up for the night, a dry bed. But she had the mental and emotional capacity of a pubescent. In school, the other kids called her retard when she walked the hallways to her special-education classes. Julie hated that. She went to three different high schools in three years, bouncing back and forth between her mother's house and her father's apartment. She dropped out in her junior year. After that, she didn't want to live with either one of her parents. She was on the streets a few months later.

Julie sat on the edge of the bed. Tom dropped heavily next to her. He was scowling.

"What's wrong with you today?" Julie asked. She screwed her face, round and flat with wide-set eyes, into her own scowl.

"None of your fucking business."

Julie started to say something back, but Tom cut her off. "I need a fucking cigarette," he said. He poked Julie in the side, beneath the ribs, the way one would tickle a baby, only harder.

Julie swatted at his hand. "Leave me alone."

Tom poked her again, aimed higher, jabbed his finger into her ribs.

She yelled it again: "Leave me alone."

Tom gave her a disgusted look, then turned away. He fished a joint out of his pocket, lit it, took a long draw, leaned back against the wall as he exhaled. He didn't have to be on the streets. Just a few years ago, he'd been living in an apartment with Norma, the mother of his twin kids, under the rumble of the interstate. She got tired of fighting with him and threw him out. He went back to see her, told her he wanted to see his kids, yelling up at her from the street. She got a restraining order, too; said he'd threatened her.

His parents would take him in, wanted to take him in,

prayed he would come home. They still lived in the house where they raised Tom and his brothers, barely two miles from the warehouse. Until a few months ago, he was the only one of their boys who wasn't locked up. His two big brothers had been locked up for almost twenty years, since that night they shot a man who happened to be in the liquor store they were robbing. And his other brother had spent most of the 1990s in prison for breaking into houses; he'd been paroled only six months earlier.

Some nights, a lot of nights, Tom's parents would drive through town looking for him. They would idle down Main Street after work, past the Victorian facades of downtown that gave way to gaudy bodegas and low-slung delis farther south. Near the corner of Charlton, they would ease off the gas, slowing to scan the faces of the drunks outside the Public Inebriate Program, which everyone called the PIP shelter. But they hardly ever saw him. It was almost as if he'd become a ghost, faded away into a netherworld. The streets his parents scoured may as well have been catacombs, a whole secret landscape of rickety shacks and damp alleys that civilians can't navigate because they can't see it, can't pick out the crevices and fissures where a man can lose himself on purpose.

And Tom had his reasons for getting lost. He was illiterate and slow-witted, not much brighter than Julie. He managed to get through high school, but he didn't learn much from the books he couldn't read. Made it hard to get a job, a good one to make enough to pay rent and utilities. On the streets, at least he could hustle when he wanted to. He could wash dishes and nail shingles to a roof and hire himself out at Preferred Labor for a few bucks a day, enough to buy his weed and some sandwiches and prepay a few minutes on his cell phone. The Mustard Seed, up on Piedmont Street, would give him a free meal, and the managers in some of the stores at the mall on the other side of the highway would let him linger inside, out of the cold or the rain, even if he wasn't buying anything. And he could usually get laid, get one of the women or girls in the same low orbit to put out.

"I want to talk," he said to Julie.

"No." She was lying across the bed, propped up on one elbow. She rubbed a crayon across the page of the coloring book opened in front of her, concentrating, being careful to stay inside the lines. "I don't want to talk to you." Her sentences had the staccato rhythm of a child. "You're smoking weed. It bothers my nose. Stay away from me."

Tom took another drag, held it, exhaled, lazy and slow. Then another. He stubbed out the roach, shifted on the bed, up onto his knees. He flashed out a hand, grabbed Julie's coloring book, tossed it to the floor. With his other hand, he grabbed her shoulder, rolled her over on her back.

"Get away from me," Julie said. "Get off of me!"

Tom put his full weight on her, pinning her to the pallet bed, grabbing at her hips.

"Get off of me," Julie said again. She pressed her hands against his chest, lifting his body enough to squirm out from beneath him. She pushed him, scrambled to a sitting position. Tom shoved her, tit for tat. She shoved him once more, hard, too. Tom lost his balance, flung a leg toward the floor to steady himself. His leg smacked the red candle, knocked it off the table. It landed in the clothes piled against the wall, disappeared into the dirty folds.

Tom caught his breath, settled back onto the bed. Julie glowered at him. He glowered back, the two of them making mean faces at each other, not saying anything.

After a moment, Julie crinkled her nose. "I smell something burning," she said.

She looked around the room. She saw a wisp of smoke curling from the corner, rising from the clothes. The pile flickered with a faint orange light, like the glow of an oversize cigarette in the dark. Julie bolted upright, leaned toward the smoldering clothing. "Look what you did," she said. "You set the clothes on fire."

Tom stared at the jumble of cotton and nylon. The first tendrils of flame sprouted in the fabric, tiny shoots unfurling. He looked at Julie, still scowling.

He got up from the bed and stomped on the clothes, trying to smother the fire with his feet. But it was almost as if he'd angered the flames, forced them to fight back to survive. A spark leaped free, landed on a scrap of paper, erupted, multiplied. Tom picked up a filthy pillow and started flailing at the fire. He was trying to beat it to death; each swing pushed a gust of fetid air into the flames. An orange tongue licked at the wooden crate, wrapped around a slat, held on. Julie kicked at the nightstand. The flames were knee-high and hungry, searching for more fuel. The pillow in Tom's hands caught fire. He dropped it onto the burning clothes.

"Get the animals," Tom said.

The cat and dog, spooked by the heat and the smoke, scurried through the door, running for somewhere to hide, somewhere to breathe. Julie couldn't grab them, couldn't herd them toward the door.

The fire spread. The blankets, the garbage, Julie's coloring book all fed the flames. Smoke stung their eyes.

"Get your shoes on," Tom said. "C'mon, get your fucking shoes on!"

Julie squished her feet into her shoes, forcing them in as she took two stumbling steps. She followed Tom through the doorway, along the hall, and down the stairs to the loading dock.

They sucked in deep breaths, cold, clear December air stinging their lungs.

Tom kept moving, Julie a few steps behind him, not saying anything. They took Franklin, passed under the highway, and walked two blocks to the Worcester Common Outlets. A third of the mall's storefronts were empty, but Media Play was still in business. Tom knew they could hang out there for a while, stay out of the cold.

Julie went all the way to the back, where the CDs are stocked. She slipped on a pair of headphones and listened to samples at a kiosk. Tom stopped in the middle, in the book section, and paced an aisle. It was hard to browse when you couldn't read. He went to get Julie.

She was fuming. "I can't believe I lost all my stuff," she said. She was practically yelling, loud enough to attract the manager's attention.

"Don't worry about it," Tom said, keeping his voice almost at a whisper, hoping to calm her down. "C'mon, let's go."

"No," she said. She stopped between the greeting cards and the computer software, planted her feet, like a toddler preparing to throw a tantrum. "I lost everything. I don't have *anything*. I lost all my stuff." She stamped her feet. "I can't believe I lost everything. *Everything*."

"Don't worry about it," Tom said again. From the corner of his eye, he saw the manager walking toward them. "Let's just go."

He guided her out of Media Play, out of the mall, out toward Main Street. They walked for fifteen minutes, to Piedmont Street. Maybe they could make it to the Mustard Seed in time for dinner. Maybe food would make her feel better.

8

THE FIRES ALWAYS SEEMED TO COME IN CLUSTERS, SHORT, SPO-
radic surges gathered around one shift or another. There was
never any pattern to it, nothing anyone could predict; in truth,
buildings burned on an almost completely random schedule.
Yet every few weeks, the haphazard order of three-tone alarms
would coincide with one of the four shifts in the Worcester Fire
Department. A kitchen would catch fire on a Wednesday night
and a cellar would smolder before dawn Friday and then the
flames would take a few days off before savaging a triple-decker
on Monday afternoon, and men from Group IV would be on
duty for all three of them. That would continue for a week or
so, Group IV getting all of the good runs, until a hiccup in the
cycle would bump the working alarms to Group II or Group I.
No one could explain why the fires seemed to work out that
way, and perhaps, if they were plotted and graphed and ana-
lyzed, they actually didn't. But it seemed like they did, and
everyone got used to the rhythm. If the last shift had been quiet,
odds are the next one would be, too.

Late autumn had been a slow stretch for Mike McNamee's
men. A handful of first-responders, an occassional call for Rescue

1, but no fires. Not in the northern half of the city, anyway. The southern district had had a couple of minor flare-ups—Main South had always burned with more frequency and intensity than the other neighborhoods—but that was District Chief Randy Chavoor's turf. And even his men hadn't seen any major action in weeks. The way things were going, nothing would catch fire until Group III came on the next night, Saturday.

For Mike, the quiet shifts weren't such a bad thing. Gave him time to catch up on his bureaucratic chores. Christmas was three weeks away, guys were looking for a few days off. At about five-thirty, Mike had gotten into his Ford Expedition to make the rounds of the northern stations, picking up the written requests for vacation time. His aide, George Zinkus, a small, wiry man with thinning hair and a choirboy's face, went with him.

At the Central Street station, Robert A. was busy with dinner, twenty-five pounds of roast beef roasting in shallow pans in the industrial oven at one end of the kitchen. Robert A. cooked for the men most nights, a skill he honed in the military and at one of his moonlight jobs, feeding the downtrodden at the PIP shelter, which he used to manage. And most nights, someone complained. If he made chowder or linguini with clams, Bert Davis would wrinkle his upper lip. "Bait," he'd say. "You're feedin' me fucking *bait*. And why do you gotta put celery in everything?" Paul Brotherton appreciated Robert A.'s pricing, though. Another guy cooked hot dogs and beans one night and jacked each man for $5.50. The next night, Robert A. grilled steaks for four bucks a head. "Christ," Paul mockingly groused. "For an extra buck-fifty we could've had franks and beans."

Dinner would be ready a few minutes after six. By the time the dishes were washed and put away, it would be going on seven o'clock, which left five hours to kill before bunking down. Paul figured he'd spend them in front of the television, settled onto one of the hand-me-down couches upstairs. The lounge was a square room in the middle of the building with a TV and VCR on a tall cart in one corner and two sofas arranged in front of it. A half-dozen more were warehoused against one wall, a graveyard of faded fabrics and ripped upholstery, old couches dumped there whenever one of the guys bought a new one for his house. When one near the TV finally deteriorated into rags, the men would haul it down to the trash and move one from the wall into its place.

If it had been a day shift, Paul could have flipped around until he tuned in Jerry Springer or Montel Williams, Paul and Tommy Dwyer cracking jokes at the screen, laughing themselves silly. Drove the other guys nuts. But there wasn't much on Friday night. Paul thought about running out to the video store.

"Go on, you've got time," Mike Coakley told him.

It was a few minutes after six o'clock. Paul, Tommy, and the captain were standing at the bottom of the back stairway, just outside the kitchen. A streetlight shone through the window.

"Nah, fuck it. I'll go after dinner," Paul said.

"Just go now. You'll be back in fifteen minutes."

"So it'll take me fifteen minutes after dinner. I want to eat first."

Coakley shrugged. "Whatever."

They heard the oven door open with a metallic squeak. Robert A. was stooped over, poking the meat with a fork. Satisfied that the beef had been roasted to a proper shade of pink, he draped a towel across his hands, grabbed the pan, and carried it to the table. The aroma of seared fat and warm meat filled the kitchen, wafted out to the apparatus floor. Men lifted their heads, scuffed their chairs against the cement as they stood up and headed toward the kitchen.

Paul ducked in the door at the far end and weaved through the bodies crowding the narrow room. He grabbed a knife from the rack above the sink and announced that he'd be doing the carving. For Paul, a routine kitchen chore could be the most dangerous part of his shift. In sixteen years on the job, five on Rescue 1 pulling people and, once, a parrot out of burning buildings, he hadn't so much as twisted an ankle. Send him into a maw of smoke and fire and he'd march out grinning. Around the station, though, he could bust himself up good. Surgeons had to sew his hand back together once after he lost control of a chopping knife in the kitchen. And he almost tanked his career two winters earlier when he slipped on a patch of ice in the back parking lot, landing so awkwardly and hard that he tore his thumb clean out of the socket. The doctor told him that without a small miracle of physical therapy, he'd have to retire. "No way," Paul said. "I'm a fireman. I'm too young to retire." He rehabilitated himself playing video games with his boys, got back to 100 percent before his first therapy session.

Now he had Yogi growling at him. He was leaning over Paul's shoulder, inspecting the neat, thin pieces Paul sliced from the roast.

"What the fuck, Brotherton," Yogi said. His walrusy mustache curled with his lip.

Paul stopped carving, looked up at him. If he'd been standing straight he would have been eye to eye with Yogi. "What?"

"What's with the fucking woman's portions? C'mon, cut it like a man, will ya?"

"What are you, the fucking portion police?"

"Yeah, if you're gonna cut it like a pussy, I'm the fucking portion police. I'm just saying, cut it—"

The first tone from the speaker interrupted him. The kitchen fell silent. Paul glanced at the clock on the wall: 6:13. A second tone, then a third. Paul put the knife down before the dispatcher spoke. Rescue always rolls on three tones.

"Striking Box 1438, Franklin and Arctic," dispatch said. The intersection was close, a quarter mile from the station. All three trucks from Central would be ordered out. The kitchen emptied, fifteen men moving toward their trucks, as dispatch read off the assignments: "Engine 1, Engine 6, Engine 12, Engine 13, Ladder 1, Ladder 5, Rescue 1, Car 3."

Most of the men had their bunker pants arranged near their spots on the truck, the legs rolled down and stuffed into their boots. In four quick motions—step through one leg, then the other, pull up the trousers, bring suspenders over the shoulders—each man was half-dressed for battle. The guys who rode in the back, behind the cab, left their coats on the seat, the sleeves threaded through the harness of a tank filled with forty-five hundred pounds of compressed air, enough for thirty minutes of relaxed breathing, fifteen of heavy panting. The drivers—Bert Davis on the ladder, Tom Dwyer on the Rescue, Charlie Murphy on the engine—would wait until they got to the scene to strap on a tank.

Twenty-five seconds after the first squawk of the alarm, the trucks were ready to go. Three diesel engines roared in synch. Bert stepped on the gas as soon as the aluminum overhead doors lifted clear of the bays. The front wheels edged onto the driveway. Mike Coakley sounded two blasts on the horn as Bert steered Ladder 1 into a wide left turn, aiming east on Central Street. Rescue 1 followed a dozen yards behind, with Engine 1 bringing up the rear, a convoy of screaming red steel and chrome.

Two blocks down Central, the caravan banked right onto Summer Street and charged into the rotary at Washington Square. Robert A., riding shotgun on Engine 1, saw a plume of smoke rising from the warehouses behind the interstate. At 6:14, he pressed the talk button on his radio, trying to raise Mike Mc-Namee. "Engine 1 to Car 3," he said. "Heavy smoke showing."

Dispatch answered, confirmed the transmission. "Engine 1, you are reporting heavy smoke showing at 18:14."

The engine followed the other two trucks under Interstate 290, then groaned to a stop in front of Worcester Cold Storage.

Robert A. jumped down from the cab directly in front of the building and turned his head toward the sky. There was nothing but clear night air above him. The stream of black smoke he'd seen from a short distance away had vanished. Maybe his perspective was off, staring up a wall of bricks too steep to bring the smoke into view. Or maybe the wind had shifted, blowing everything over the back side. Or maybe the old warehouse had sucked the whole cloud inside, as if it was holding back a secret.

"What the fuck," he muttered to no one in particular. "Hey—which fuckin' building's on fire?"

Randy Chavoor left South Station, the base of operations for his district, at six o'clock to take care of some niggling matters at headquarters on Grove Street. His aide, Franny Baldino, drove him in Car 4, the Expedition assigned to the district chief commanding the southern end of the city. On the way, they passed Worcester Cold Storage, which lies just north of the line dividing the two fire districts. From the street in front of the warehouse just after six, neither fireman noticed anything unusual about the building.

The drive to Grove Street took less than ten minutes. Randy got out of the Expedition and entered through the garage, greeting a few of the guys as he crossed the apparatus floor, and cut through a back passageway into the complex of administrative offices. At 6:12, he heard Maggie, one of the women who works in the alarm center, calling him on the radio. She wanted to know if Box 1438, Franklin and Arctic, was in the southern district.

He knew it wasn't, but it was close enough to steal the call. He knew his buddy Mike McNamee would do the same thing, grab an alarm from him if he had half a chance. His pulse quickened as he reached for his radio, and an impish smirk creased his cheek. He pushed the talk button. "Uh, yeah, Maggie, I'm on it."

No answer, as if she didn't even hear him. He fiddled with his radio, gave it a closer look, clicked the button a couple times. He realized the battery was dead. She hadn't heard him. Damn it. He glanced around, spotted a phone, took two steps toward it. Maggie came back on the air. "Car 4, disregard."

Randy let out an exasperated sigh. "Ah, shit."

Mike NcNamee and George Zinkus were on the far edge of their district, near the Greendale Station three miles north of Central Street, when the alarm went off. As the third tone sounded, Mike cocked his head toward the radio, listening for the address. "Striking Box 1438 . . ."

He turned toward George, lowered his brow, looked at him over the top of his glasses. Mike knew the address from memory, knew exactly which building rang 1438. "Bad building," he said.

George nodded, repeated it with him. "*Bad building.*"

"Is that Randy's or ours?" Mike asked. "I think that's ours. Is that our last box?"

George grinned. "Ah, Randy'll take it."

Then dispatch read the truck assignments. All of Central Street. Definitely northern district. Mike hit the lights and siren, and George punched the gas. He slowed at the edge of Knight Square, then accelerated down Burncoat Street to the ramp for I-290. Mike estimated they'd be on scene two minutes after the first units. With any luck, they could clear out within an hour. "Please let this be a little shit fire," he whispered to himself. "Just a shitty little fire, please."

The radio caught his attention. "Fire Alarm to Car 3."

"Car 3."

"Chief, be advised that an off-duty P.O. states smoke coming from the building. He is up on the highway and sees smoke coming from the top of the building."

"Received."

Eleven seconds later, four blocks from the highway entrance, Mike heard Robert A. radio that he, too, saw heavy smoke showing. Mike's stomach tightened. He grabbed the radio. "Fire Alarm, be aware that Car 3 is responding from Greendale."

"Fire Alarm has that."

George wheeled onto the interstate and squashed the pedal to the floor. Two minutes later, at the spot where the highway rises above downtown, Mike got his first look at the warehouse, an aerial view, his line of sight almost even with the top of the building. A column of charcoal smoke curled from the roof. He felt another pinch in his gut. From that angle, the fire didn't appear to be particularly menacing. But it had gotten at least a short head start on his men, staked a claim somewhere in that massive edifice. From the outside it was impossible to guess how bad the inside might be. The first alarm had come in only four minutes ago, but Mike didn't want to risk being caught short of men and equipment.

"Car 3 to Fire Alarm."

"Fire Alarm answering Car 3."

"We're just getting off I-290 right now," Mike said. "Strike the second alarm. We're going to have the second alarm companies stage until we have a place for them."

"Fire Alarm has that."

Three more tones sounded in stations across the city. Three more trucks—Engine 16 out of Grove Street, and Engine 2 and Aerial Scope 2 from South Division—were on the road in less than a minute. All three were understaffed: between them, they carried only ten men, a third short of a full complement. But having ten more able bodies waiting on the sidelines gave Mike a small measure of comfort.

He was out of the Expedition, standing just outside the building, trying to get a read on it. A dozen men were inside, searching for flames that were hiding deep in the bowels, somewhere behind the solid brick walls. With no open windows, there was no telltale glow, no bright orange marker to give away the fire to the men on the street. It could be in a corner or in the middle or everywhere and on the first floor or the third or the fourth. Mike scanned the walls again. He realized he couldn't even tell how many floors were in the warehouse.

He clicked on his radio. "Franklin Command to the second alarm companies. I want you to stage under 290 until you hear from me. Just stage under 290 until you hear from me."

"Engine 16 has that."

"Scope 2 has that."

"Engine 2."

"All companies stage on Franklin Street," Mike said again. "Back away until we get a handle on this."

He started toward a corner door, then stopped, looked up at the warehouse again, up into the sky. The smoke was still lazy, no worse than a factory smoke stack on the swing shift. Mike put his radio back to his mouth.

"Command to Fire Alarm," he said. "Do we have any building information on this?"

A three-second pause before the reply: "I'm checking, Chief."

Jay Lyons jumped from his seat in the Grove Street station when the second alarm sounded, three tones pricking his adrenal gland. On instinct, an overeager reflex, he took a hurried step toward Engine 3 before dispatch assigned any units.

Randy Chavoor chortled at him, brought Jay up short. "C'mon," he said. "Sit down. You don't go on the second—it's 2 and 16."

A sheepish grin crept over Jay's face. "Yeah," he said. "I knew that."

Randy chuckled again. He liked Jay, admired his enthusiasm. Good fireman. He'd get his chance. Everyone did eventually.

9

MIKE HAD BEEN IN BAD BUILDINGS BEFORE. MORE THAN HE could count, and each dodgy in its own particular way. Some were dangerous because of they way they'd been constructed, like that warehouse on Jacques Street, with its reinforced storerooms and heat-sealing fire doors. Cellars, stone-walled pits with only one way in or out, were always risky. In the 1970s and 1980s, arsonists booby-trapped triple-deckers with plastic bags filled with gasoline tucked between the ceiling joists, little bombs that kept the fire spreading. A man pulling down plaster, if he wasn't careful, could get ten gallons of fuel dumped on his head.

Sometimes a building went bad for reasons no one could predict. There were too many variables in a fire. Maybe the flames would tickle a hidden stash of propane or maybe the wind would shift direction or maybe the rafters were rotted with age and moisture and would burn away twice as fast as the men chopping through the roof had guessed. Sometimes, the fire just got a head start, ran wild before the engines, ladders, and rescue could scream out of their stations, devoured the walls and the floors and the furniture, turned everything orange and hot and black and choking. Sometimes the men had to stand back, let the flames feed, corral the fire with the spray from a dozen hoses until there was nothing left to burn.

The worst fire in Worcester, Massachusetts, the inferno that killed the most people, eleven civilians, happened in the hours before dawn on July 11, 1973. Mike was a rookie, six months on the job, working Ladder 7 out of the Winslow Street station, a decrepit old wreck a few blocks west of downtown. There had been a shower late the night before, a light and misty rain, not hard enough to wash away the sticky summer heat. In a flophouse at 728 Main Street, five stories framed from timbers cut a hundred years earlier and faced in brick, the tenants kept their windows open to the breeze that blew in from the west. They were poor folks and low-rung working stiffs, janitors and transient laborers, aged shut-ins and welfare cases, the same demographic mix as the rest of Main South. People paying nineteen bucks a week to a flophouse landlord didn't get air-conditioning.

At about two-thirty on the morning of July 11, two teenage girls climbed a wooden porch attached to the second floor on the backside of 728 Main. Below them was an alley and, if they looked off the porch toward the horizon, the breeze would have brushed against their faces. Each one had a can filled with gasoline, which they splashed around the decking, and matches, which they lit and tossed into the puddles. Fire raced across the porch, a jagged seam of orange flitting and twisting on a blue cushion of hot gas, almost as if it were floating, hovering a centimeter above the floor. A tentacle of flame licked at the railing, then bit, found a hold, and started to climb. A lovely sight, beautiful and hypnotizing. They wanted to see the porch burn, but only the porch, wanted to watch the tangerine flickers and sparks, to gawk at the firemen who would stomp up the stairs with their hoses and axes, the night and the alley throbbing red and white.

Such fires were not unusual in Main South. Firemen on that side of Worcester had scrambled from one scene to the next for months, starting one night in February when a surly drinker threw a Molotov cocktail at a waitress in Longo's Lounge. From then on, it seemed that something was always burning, and quite often several things at once. On one day in April, two kids lit up an abandoned flophouse, a toddler with a pack of matches burned up his family's apartment, a bathroom was set on fire at 667 Main Street, followed by a garage on Charlton Street. The rooming houses on Main were favorite targets: the building across the street from 728 was destroyed on May 27, and the rear porches on the one next door had been set on fire twice that spring.

But this one, a kicky little arson on a run-down deck, over-ran the building. The wind from the west pushed the flames toward the brick facade, fed them fresh oxygen, teased them higher. At an open window, the fire reached inside, felt for something to cling to, grabbed hard and pulled itself in. Then it nearly exploded. The interior turned into a blast furnace, fresh air huffing through the windows, the bricks holding in the heat, the two forces complementing each other, the flames mating and multiplying. Five minutes before three o'clock, as the heat shattered glass and smoke clogged hallways, tenants started choking awake. The flames were already eating through the roof.

The first alarm came in at 2:59. Mike and the rest of the Winslow Street shift bolted out of their bunks. Mike had just cleared the pole down to the apparatus floor when the second alarm was sounded. He pulled on his boots and hauled himself onto Ladder 7, the truck already rumbling. The rear wheels hadn't hit the blacktop on the street when a third alarm was sounded. The fourth and fifth—which signify hellfire has been loosed on earth—were struck twelve minutes after the first, at 3:11.

The first engines on the scene tapped hydrants on the far side of the alley behind the building. But by then the fire had too much of an advantage. The rear was a sheet of flame, a lavish curtain that rose from the pavement, up the wall and eighty feet beyond, lighting a bank of smoke held low by the humidity. The fire had spread so far so fast that half the tenants never had time to stumble down the stairways. A few found ladders made from metal links or knotted rope in boxes beneath their windows. The rest were dangling from ledges or leaning over the sills, weighing the odds of surviving a multistory drop against the odds of being incinerated. Alexander Shemeth was one of those trying to decide, trapped in his fifth-floor apartment. He was sixty years old and everyone called him Hooks, on account of the prosthetics that had replaced the hands that were blown off by a dynamite cap twenty-one years earlier. He couldn't force his way through the smoke in the hallway, but he couldn't last much longer in his room, either. So he climbed through the window, twisted around until his chest was flush with the building, and set his hooks into the sill. He could operate a factory blowtorch with those hooks, could even cook with them. Maybe he could hang from a piece of limestone with them, too.

The hooks held to the ledge, but not to the man. When Ladder 7 pulled up to 728 Main, Hooks was crumpled on the ground, dead. The first thing Mike saw were the prosthetics, still dangling from the sill four stories above, wobbling against the building like small cornices that had broken loose.

People, backlit from the flames, screamed from almost every window above the second floor, their faces disappearing behind a draft of smoke, reappearing, vanishing again. A firefighter on the back of Ladder 1 scanned the upper floors, calculating who was in the most peril, steering the truck's long, steel arm from one window to the next. "Hang on," he screamed. "Don't jump. Do not jump. I'm comin' to get you. Just hang on."

Mike was scared. He'd been in dozens of fires already, but only small ones, one alarms, two at most. Never something like this, something this bad, rampaging, voracious. "Lieutenant," he asked his boss, "are people gonna die here tonight?"

Walter Rydzewski barely looked at him, too focused on the job. "They already have, kid," he said.

The two of them grabbed a thirty-five-foot ladder and started toward the left side of the building, moving at a quick trot. Mike kept pace with Rydzewski, the ladder heavy on his shoulder. Halfway down the alley, he saw a blur of downward movement from the corner of his eye, just at the edge of his peripheral vision. A dull smack came next. Mike stopped short. A middle-aged woman lay on the pavement, mangled, her legs bent unnaturally beneath her torso, all of her still and quiet.

Mike tried to take a step toward her. Rydzewski felt the tug on the ladder, turned, barked. "What are you doin'?" he snapped, sounding both annoyed and incredulous.

"I'm trying to help her," Mike said.

"What are you, nuts?" the lieutenant yelled at the rookie. "Forget her. She's down." He jerked his head up and over his left shoulder, flung his arm toward the people wailing from the higher windows. "They're not. Let's go."

Mike swallowed hard, then turned away. He matched his steps with Rydzewski's, the two of them humping down the alley to a spot where they could raise the ladder. He knew his lieutenant was right. A fire scene, like a battlefield, sometimes demands triage. There is no sense in trying to save the ones already out of danger. Once a body is out of the building, regardless of how it got there or in what condition, it becomes a concern for the medics. In any case, no one can save the dead.

Worcester firemen got twenty-two people out of 728 Main Street that night. For the next thirty minutes, they moved ladders along the perimeter of the building, setting them against the searing bricks, one man climbing up into the smoke and coming back down with a body slung over his shoulder. After the left side was clear, Mike was routed to the other end on a crew working a forty-five-foot ladder, one so long that it requires men to use long rods, called tormentor poles, to guide the tip into place. Once the ladder is raised, two men—or one if they're short-staffed, which the Worcester Fire Department was in the middle of the July vacation season—haul on a rope to raise the extension. Metal clasps, called pawls, eventually catch a rung to lock the whole contraption in place.

A young voice, a teenager at most, yelled from above. The ladder crew couldn't see through the smoke, couldn't see where the screams came from. They triangulated by the sound, put the forty-five-footer beneath where it seemed to be the loudest, and started raising, clipping the poles into place.

"Get rid of those fucking poles!" The district chief was next to them, hollering orders. "Put the poles down and get that fucking ladder up."

The tormentors hit the ground and the ladder was manhandled into position, brute strength and adrenaline forcing it up. Less stable, less precise, but faster. Smoke swallowed the tip. Mike pulled on the rope, wrestling the extension. He felt a tug, then a deadweight. The ladder started to tip, lurching twenty degrees to one side. Someone, the screaming kid, was on it. The clasps hadn't set. The extension started to slide down. Mike fought the weight from above. "Get on this thing," Mike yelled. "Someone get on this, the pawls aren't locked. The fucking pawls aren't locked!"

Another set of hands grabbed the rope, held it firm, pulled. A firefighter named Dennis Collins flashed past them, put his boot on the first rung, scrambled up into the cloud. As soon as he touched him, the kid passed out cold. Dennis caught him, lugged him to the ground.

Once the windows had been cleared of survivors, the lieutenant from Rescue 1 grabbed him by the arm. "I want you to come with me," he said, leading Mike toward the front door. The rescue guys were working the inside of the building, like they usually do, crawling through the smoke and flames searching for anyone who couldn't get to a window. It was perilous work, performed without a hose or a ladder. Rookies normally didn't work the rescue squad.

Mike followed the lieutenant and two other firefighters up the stairs to the third floor. The clouds, dark as a new-moon midnight, wrapped around him like a steaming sheet, and the heat forced every man down to his knees, almost to his belly. Just inside the hallway, maybe six feet from the stairs, the lieutenant leaned in close to Mike. "I want you to stay here," he shouted, straining his throat to force the words over the roar. "Turn your light on"—each man had a lamp powered by a brick-size battery clipped to his belt—"and stay in this doorway."

Mike nodded, switched on the light by his belly. He was going to be the beacon man, the faint point of white shining through the smoke. The rescue guys crawled off into the murk, and Mike was alone in an inferno. The sound was deafening, as if a thousand thunderheads had dropped from the sky and surrounded him, enveloped him, and erupted all at once, rumbling and popping and snapping. He waited only five minutes, maybe six, long enough for the point men to scuttle through a handful of small rooms and follow his light back to the stairs, but it seemed like an hour. He cursed himself. "Shit," he thought. "What the fuck have you gotten yourself into?" He considered the fact that he could actually die, choking on poison or screaming from third-degree burns.

He hustled down the stairs with the rescue crew, gulped fresh air, wiped smears of sweat and ash across his brow. Then he was sent back inside, this time with Dennis Collins and a squad from Engine 4. They were ordered up to the second floor, where the fire was rooted in rooms that ran down both sides of a narrow hallway. They took up a position a few feet down the corridor, between two doors, one on the left and one on the right, that opened into small rooms howling with flames, fire so dense it appeared as solid, writhing blocks. The nozzle man pivoted to the right and opened the flow. Hundreds of gallons a minute poured into the first room, a torrent that took four men to control. They moved the nozzle in a pattern, sweeping it up, then down, over a few inches, up, down, washing the entire room with cold water.

Finally, the fire cooled, blacked out, the hot orange replaced by heavy smoke. The men on the hose pivoted left and opened the nozzle into the opposite room. Up, down, over, up, down, over. Then, behind them, a rush of boiling heat and the fast, deep whoosh of an explosion. The room they'd just finished washing had reignited, the smoke catching fire from the smoldering heat.

The men held their ground, battling both fronts, washing one room, then the next, then twisting back to attack the one that had blown up again. There was a crack in the air above them, a bang that broke through the drone of the fire. A fiery beam collapsed through the ceiling, crashing down on Dennis. A glancing blow, enough to cut him but not knock him off his feet. He shook it off. He was the senior man on the floor, an ex-marine, disciplined, brave but not foolish enough to stay in a fight he was clearly losing.

"Hey, we're not gonna win in here," he hollered. "We gotta start backing out. C'mon, back it out."

"No, we can do it," one of the men shouted back. "We can do this."

"No, we can't," Dennis repeated. "Let's go. Back it out."

The commanders on the scene were already ordering the building evacuated. With the roof already collapsed and fire everywhere else, there was too much of a risk of another floor giving way, of a man getting disoriented in the fog. All the men fell back to a defensive perimeter, aimed their hoses at 728 Main, and opened them up. "Surround and drown," they call it. Put the wet stuff on the red stuff until the red stuff gives up.

The red stuff gave up soon enough. The main fire was out by four o'clock, a little more than an hour after the first alarm had sounded. But it seemed like an eternity to Mike. And the night wasn't even close to being over. There were hot spots, stubborn pockets of fire, that needed to be hit up close. And the bodies had to be dug out of the rubble. The firemen found nine corpses that night. The tenth would be recovered almost a week later, buried beneath bricks and charred timbers in the basement. And the eleventh was Olivine Moxley, who was so badly injured when she jumped from a third-floor window that she never got out of the hospital before she died four years later.

An hour after dawn, the pace finally slowed enough that some of the men could take a short break, at least get off their feet. Six of them worked one of the last hot spots, soaking down a pile of embers on the fourth floor for thirty minutes. When the fire was out, they were ordered down a ladder on the south side of the building. Ronald Paradis hauled himself through the window and started feeling his way down the rungs. Above him, three men waited for him to clear the ladder. Below him, in front of the building, Mike was lowering himself onto the rear plate of Ladder 7, thankful to finally sit.

Then a snap, like a desiccated bone cracking in two. Mike looked up. The south wall was collapsing from the second floor up, tumbling into the alley. Paradis looked up. A brick plummeted toward his face. He lunged for the hose dangling next to the ladder, grabbed it hard, pulled it into his chest. The brick hit him square in the face. He hung on, unconscious but instinctive, and slid to the ground. Two firemen broke his fall.

Paul Belculfine reached for a beam as the floor fell out from under his feet, caught it with one hand and one leg, like a cowboy who couldn't quite right himself on his horse. Rubble rained down, smashing his face, breaking his cheekbones. Still, he hung on for almost three minutes, until two men could carry him down a ladder.

The two other men on the fourth floor, Danny O'Keefe and Lt. Russell Perry, dropped with the building, the remnants of the wall avalanching on top of them. They were buried for almost five minutes before their comrades dug them out.

Mike, like everyone else, jerked toward the alley. "Everybody out!" the commanding officer yelled, stopping all of them short. "Only rescue guys. I want everyone else out." Once part of a building goes, there's no telling what else is waiting to fall. The idea is to limit the exposure, to not risk wounding, or killing, more men than necessary. The rescue guys could get their brethren out.

No firemen died that night. But Perry and Belculfine both retired within a year. And before the collapse, seven other firefighters were hurt. Any one of them could have died, some of them probably should have died, spared only by fate and their friends.

When he went home later that morning, Mike was too wired to sleep. Maybe it was the adrenaline still running through his veins. He replayed every awful scene in his head, tried to distill each into a lesson. They all meshed into one, a single truism that isn't obvious until it is observed. Fire is capricious. It can move faster and more furiously than any human being, no matter how well trained or well armed. "If you're in its way," Mike told himself, "it's gonna take you."

The sun was almost down before his eyes closed and he collapsed into a deep, exhausted sleep.

10

BY THE TIME MIKE HAD STRUCK THE SECOND ALARM FOR Worcester Cold Storage, a dozen of his men already were forcing their way inside to search for the flames. Ladder 5 was in front of the building, its big stick already rising to the roof, two men climbing it. Ladder 1 was around the corner from Franklin Street on Arctic, parked parallel to the side of the building with its ladder, 110 feet of high-tensile aluminum, stretched from the turntable on the back. Capt. Mike Coakley and Bert Davis had scrambled up, moving quickly but not frantically. Two other men on Ladder 1, Yogi and John Casello, followed the loading dock to a steel door located in the middle. Most of Rescue 1 hustled up behind them. Paul Brotherton held a flashlight while Yogi forced open the door.

To simplify things in the chaos, firefighters reduced the contours of every building to the first four letters of the alphabet, starting with "A" in front and moving clockwise around the structure. That made Franklin Street the A wall and Arctic B. Robert A. ordered his men to tap a hydrant at the A-B corner, running two three-inch lines from the water main into the pumper. Then Robert A. grabbed another one of his men and headed down the B side to the door Yogi had busted open.

Eight men stepped into a dark and narrow vestibule at the bottom of a stairwell. They could make out a faint smell of smoke through the stink of rotting garbage and human waste, but the air was clear. Six of them turned toward the stairs. Robert A. was leading. He stopped on the second-floor landing, pushed open the door, and stuck his head in, a quick spot-check. No fire. He hustled up to the third floor, did the same thing, then started climbing again. Lt. Dave Halvorsen and Charlie Rogacz, the engine man working overtime on Rescue 1, stopped to do a more thorough search on three.

"Dave, we're going to the roof with the cap'n," Paul Brotherton said, meaning himself and Jerry Lucey.

"Got it," the lieutenant said as he disappeared through the door with Charlie.

Robert A. peeked for fire on three more landings. The stairs came to a dead end at a rooftop bulkhead. He forced it open, then climbed up into the open air. Standing on top, it was easier to figure out the rough dimensions of the warehouse, see how it was put together. It was actually two buildings, one a square eighty-eight feet to a side and the other a rectangle, seventy-two feet deep by one hundred twenty feet long, the two of them fused together into the shape of a stubby capital "L" by a common firewall that poked up like a short parapet. Robert A. and the rest of the men had emerged on the square part, near the B edge. To their right was a skylight, glass reinforced with wire mesh, that capped an elevator shaft.

They crossed the roof, hopped over the firewall. Another skylight, identical to the first, fifteen feet by fifteen feet, sat off-center, closer to the C wall. An obvious vent. Robert A. turned to Brotherton and Jerry Lucey. "Clean it out," he told them.

Jerry held a flathead ax. Paul was carrying his weapon of

choice, a Haligan, the same tool he always took into battle. It was a rod of tempered steel roughly the size of a baseball bat with one end flattened into a two-pronged claw. At the other end, attached at ninety-degree angles to the shaft, were a flat wedge that could slip between a door and a jamb to pry it open and a pear-size steel point that could puncture almost anything Paul swung it at.

The glass shattered with the first jab from the Haligan. A puff of black smoke coughed through the hole. Jerry and Paul kept working, tearing away the mesh, opening a vent the size of a cramped family room. More smoke wheezed from the hole.

Six stories down, Yogi and John Casello were searching the first floor. When everyone else had gone up, they had pushed through the vestibule into the main part of the warehouse, which was huge and empty. Years before, when the Worcester Cold Storage was in business, forklifts had rolled through there, hauling pallets to the freight elevator just off the B wall, so they could be lifted to the meat lockers and refrigerators above. Now it was just a massive, moldering cave.

The ladder men explored the dark, following their flashlights to a brick wall on the far side. No sign of flames. They backtracked toward the door, and went up three short, twisting risers of black steel to the second floor. Instead of an open vault, they stepped into a small chamber approximately fifteen feet wide and twenty-five feet deep. There were steel doors, each with a heavy, circular handle that lay flush inside a pocket, on the side walls that led into large storage lockers. At the far end of the chamber was an identical door. Yogi pulled it open and walked into a third storeroom. It was a massive space, broken every few yards by sixteen-inch columns that held up the floor above. If the lights had still worked, it would have appeared reasonably uncluttered, like a sparsely but evenly wooded forest of square timbers. In the pitch black, though, it would be a maze, the columns seemingly walls, each corner bending into another phantom corridor.

Yogi heard the fire before he could see it, a ferocious popping and snapping, muffled but still close. He kept walking until he reached the firewall, then moved to his left, toward the back of the building. The sounds grew louder. His light caught the outline of a door through the bricks. He nudged at it, expecting it to crack enough to give him a look inside.

The door swung open, away from Yogi, as if a spring inside had jerked it back. A fierce wave of heat rushed out, took his breath away. The room beyond the door was nothing but fire, orange flames writhing thick as jungle grass. It was like standing in front of an incinerator, a blast furnace.

"Hey, Johnny," he called over his shoulder. "C'mere and take a look at this fucking thing."

Casello sucked in his breath.

"That's some serious shit, huh?" Yogi was grinning. There was a lot of fire in that small room. Enough fire for everyone. He reached for his radio.

Mike McNamee was striding toward the A-B corner of the warehouse when one of the men from Engine 13 called him on the radio. Those guys had found the fire at the same time as Yogi, but from the opposite angle, having come up to the second floor via a stairwell on the C side of the warehouse.

"Thirteen to Command. The fire is in the elevator shaft on the second and third floor."

"Ten-four," Mike radioed back. "Is it localized or is it getting out?"

Yogi keyed his microphone before Engine 13 could answer. "Ladder 100 to Command," he said. "Urgent."

"Go ahead Ladder 1."

"This is Ladder 1. I'm on the second floor and I'm in a freezer room, and I've got a room full of fire up here. I need a line on the second floor."

"Received."

That was good news. Only seven minutes after the alarm went off, the fire was located and essentially contained. Mike knew men were on the roof, which meant they had more than likely punched at least one hole through it. Mike took another step and his radio crackled again.

"Rescue 600 to Command." It was Jerry Lucey. "We're up at the roof. We have heavy smoke and embers showing." The puffs and wispy streams had turned into a rushing contrail, roiling and oily and flecked with glowing orange highlights. But that was all right, too. At twenty minutes after six o'clock, everything was going the way it was supposed to. The men had entered, vented, and now they were beginning to attack. Routine, the same operation they'd executed a thousand times before.

With Casello downstairs helping gather the hoses, Yogi tried to pull the door closed, keep the fire contained until they could get some water on it. He had to lean back, put his considerable weight into the effort, fight against the draft that dragged the door toward the flames. The physics were all wrong: the heat should have been pushing the door out, away from the flames, not creating a whirlwind draft rushing into the fire.

Robert A. found Yogi wrestling with the door a few moments later. He'd tromped down from the roof after the skylight had been smashed out, then detoured into the second floor when he heard the radio transmissions.

"Hey, Yogi," he said, "that don't look too good." His tone was mock worry, his grammar deliberately garbled for effect.

"No, it don't," Yogi said. "Come and look what I found." He

was still smiling, playful, like a kid who'd just found a steep and bumpy hill to roll down on his bike. Sure, it looked dangerous. But that was the fun of it.

He gave Robert A. a look into the room, then wrenched the door closed again. Within seconds, four other men arrived with the hoses, a pair of two-and-a-half-inch lines and one inch-and-three-quarter line. It took a moment to charge them all, to get water from the engines up two floors and across the ware-house to the nozzle.

"Better put your masks on, boys," Yogi said once the lines were charged. He was still grinning. "This could get ugly."

He let the door swing open and stepped toward the flames with a hose. The shutoff valve on the smaller line got snagged on something screwed to the wall just inside the doorway, taking one hose out of commission. With the two larger ones, the men moved to their right, spraying a deluge into the fire, almost five hundred gallons a minute between them. They knocked down the first bank of flames quickly enough, then advanced through a burned-out doorway to a second front.

The fire in there was more intense, a howling orange wind. The hoses were useless against gases so hot; the streams of water were vaporized into steam a few inches out of the nozzle, then whooshed away by flames that moved like the afterburners of a jet, streaked with cobalt blue and screaming horizontally into the elevator shaft, following a wide path to the vent in the roof.

The heat was eating through the ceiling, melting away the staples and the joists that held the electrical system in place. Yogi was near the firewall, trying to advance the line, when a tangle of wires fell from above, knocked him off balance. He wobbled, stumbled, fell backward, through the doorway, landing flat with a view of the ceiling. Above him, he saw something strange. Smoke was streaming *into* the fire, like the ribbons of a thunderhead racing into a funnel cloud. He stared at it for a second or two, perplexed. "Hey, Cap," he hollered to Robert A. "Something don't look right. Everything's moving the wrong way."

He got to his feet. He wondered how much air he had left in his tank. Reinforcements, a fresh crew of firemen, were on the way to relieve the guys handling the hoses. Yogi headed for the door, going down for a new bottle of air.

At 6:23, Mike McNamee was making his way into the ground floor of the warehouse for a firsthand look at the conditions. His men were radioing updates from all over the building, telling him where the fire was burning, how it was moving. George Zinkus told him there was heavy fire showing at the C-D corner, where the cold storage offices used to be, one of two areas of the building with windows cut through the exterior walls. The flames weren't spreading outward, though, just burning up into the elevator shaft. Mike Coakley, up on the roof, reported that a swirl of embers was rushing out through the open skylight.

So far, so good. The blaze was contained in the center of the building, the heat and the smoke blowing straight up through the vent. He had five hoses moving into position, three from the B stairs and two from the C side, effectively surrounding the flames. And nothing was spreading. Mike was about fifty feet from the firewall, coming from the entrance on Arctic Street, and he could hear the fire and smell the smoke. But the air wasn't noticeably warm, and it was still clear, not even enough stray vapors to sting his eyes or scratch his throat. The only thing that struck him as unusual was how bright the inside was on that floor.

He saw Mike Conley, the captain from Engine 13, and one of his men dragging a two-and-a-half-inch across the warehouse, toward the stairs on the C side. "Just cool the shaft," Mike told the captain. "We don't want to lose the stairs."

He heard his call sign on the radio. Fire Alarm trying to raise him. He pressed the talk button. "Go ahead, Fire Alarm."

"Command, be advised that a citizen just reported to a police officer that there may be two people that live in that building."

"Received."

Mike wasn't concerned. He knew the rescue teams would be searching the building as a matter of course. Rescue men always assumed someone could be lost inside, and they kept looking until the heat or the smoke forced them out. Twenty minutes after the first alarm, most of Worcester Cold Storage seemed less menacing than the average house fire. Away from the actual flames, none of the men had even bothered to put their masks on.

For the next few minutes, Mike kept in contact with the engine crews trying to position the lines. Engine 16 tapped a dead hydrant, which required rerouting a water supply through another pumper. He keyed his radio again. "Engine 2, can you feed a couple of lines into their lines from the next nearest hydrant?"

"Chief, the next available hydrant is across Grafton Street, so we'd have to block Grafton."

Mike considered the logistics, tying up a main access road. Engine 2 radioed again. "Do you want me to lay it across Grafton?"

"No," Mike said, "I'm going to send you around the other way. You're going to have to go up the long way. Ladder 5 is blocking here. You have to go up and over Wall Street, come back down, lay down."

A minor annoyance. A short delay in getting some more wet stuff on the red stuff. But nothing critical.

Eight minutes had gone by since Fire Alarm passed on the report of people living in the building. Mike figured it was time to ask for a status report. "Command to Rescue."

"Rescue." It was Dave Halvorsen.

"Rescue, did you check the rumor that we have a couple of homeless people living at the rear of this building?"

"Checked the second and third floor," Dave replied. "Found nothing, Chief. We're moving our way up."

Another six minutes ticked by. Outside, trucks lumbered through the streets, men screwed connections onto hydrants. Every line was charged, Engine 1 had plenty of water to spare, Engine 2 ended up feeding only its own lines.

At 6:38, Dave Halvorsen called Mike again. "Rescue to Command," he said.

"Command, go ahead." Mike had worked his way up to the third floor, where the conditions were the same as the first, only a vague haze of smoke.

"Chief, we're up on the fourth floor. We can hear fire crackling, but we can't see anything. We are in the rear of the building, on the C side."

Mike misheard the transmission, felt a shudder of worry. "Did you say you have more fire on the fourth floor?"

"We can hear the fire crackling, but we can't see any fire at all. But we can hear it."

That sounded better. Relief pushed away the dread. "Okay," Mike said. "That's because it's running right up the shaft."

Mike moved into the vestibule on the third floor. He pushed through another door, deeper into the warehouse. His eyes followed the beam of his light, picking out the columns. In the gloom, the room looked like a labyrinth. A million bad secrets could be hidden in there. He got on the radio again. "Interior to Fire Alarm."

"Fire Alarm."

"Put out an emergency broadcast to all companies operating inside to use extreme caution," he said. "There could be holes in the floor, and to use extreme caution as they are moving."

"Received."

He heard alert tones over his radio, then Fire Alarm repeating his warning. He took a few more steps, then stopped, considered his own advice. Unlike the men looking for homeless tramps or the guys spraying water, he was alone, wandering deeper into a burning building with no hose to lead him back if things turned bad, no partner to watch his back. And Halvorsen and one of his men had searched this floor a few minutes earlier. Mike knew they'd been thorough. He decided to retreat to the stairs.

He turned around. In front of him were three identical doors. His felt his stomach tighten. He opened all three doors, one at a time. Behind each, he saw another room. *Shit.* He retraced his steps in his mind. *Through two doors, left, straight, right, stop, turn around, left, straight, right.* He should have been back where he started. His gut twitched again. *This is bad.* He took a deep breath, steadied his nerves. *Just listen. It's gotta be one of these.* He stood stone still, even held his breath for a long moment, focusing on the smothered sounds of boots clomping up stairs, men hollering, axes and Haligans bouncing against railings and walls. He cocked his head toward each door in turn. The noise seemed louder through the middle one, but barely. He reached for the handle.

Mike played his light across the walls of the room behind the door. On the far side, the beam slid across another door, one that looked the same as every other one. He tried that one. It led into the vestibule, which seemed familiar. He scanned the perimeter, found the stairs behind a cement partition. If he'd blinked, he would have missed them.

He let out a heavy breath when he reached the steps, felt a chill in his spine. Firemen were trained to keep their bearings even in total darkness. In most buildings, they could follow the walls because they always led to a window or a door. If that didn't work, they would keep track of their movements, remember the number of steps and direction of each turn. Mike had done that hundreds of times before, crawled miles through blinding black. This time, upright and guided by a flashlight, he was fumbling through a funhouse of matching doors and shifting angles. Creepy building. He decided to check the fourth floor, but not go in as far.

11

A MILE AND HALF FROM THE BURNING WAREHOUSE, IN THE Grove Street station, Lt. John Sullivan kept his attention on the radio, monitoring the progress of the attack through the static-fractured chatter. He wasn't terribly concerned. All the voices were calm, controlled, no edge of concern in anyone's tone or phrasing. It sounded like a messy fire, an unpredictable rogue. But it was under control. Other than the single dead hydrant that had forced McNamee to reposition trucks, the battle was going as smoothly as any such firefight could.

Lt. Tom Spencer crossed the apparatus floor at about six-thirty. Three men from Grove Street, all on Engine 16, had rolled out the door thirteen minutes earlier when the second alarm had been struck, and he noticed some of the other guys were getting antsy. He saw Sullivan, the lieutenant on Engine 3, fiddling with his gear next to the passenger side of the truck. Sully stepped through one leg of his pants and into one boot, then the other, pulled the suspenders up, dipped a shoulder through one loop.

"What are you doing?" Tom asked. He said it with a teasing sneer.

"Just getting ready," Sullivan said. Sully knew. He'd already told Jay Lyons: *Three alarms. I can smell it.* "Always gotta be ready, you know."

Tommy let out a good-natured laugh, shook his head as Sully snapped the suspenders over his other shoulder. He liked Sully, mostly because he knew him outside of the station—their teenage daughters were best friends, and one of them was always driving his girl to the other one's house. One on one, away from the job, Sully was a good guy. He had his problems in the station, though. They held the same rank, and had for six years. Tom always hoped Sully would learn from watching him, figure out how to lead his men without pushing them, exert his authority by example rather than bluster. Maybe it was the age difference, Sully's youth getting in the way. Tom had been on the job almost twice as long, since 1979, had worked his way up slowly. When Sully made lieutenant in 1983, he was the youngest officer in the department, only six years behind him. Some of the guys thought he overcompensated, barked out orders so no one would forget the young guy was in charge.

If a third alarm was struck, Tom was ready. He felt his medallion against his chest. It was a silver icon of St. Florian, the patron saint of firefighters. Now there was a saint a man could get behind. Florian was a Roman soldier and a closet Christian in the second century who, according to legend, once saved an entire town from burning by throwing a single bucket of water on the flames. But he fell out of favor with the emperor because he refused to slaughter his fellow Christians or renounce his faith. He was whipped, flayed alive, and set on a pile of kindling to be burned to death. "If you burn me," he told his executioners, "I will climb to heaven on the flames." So the soldiers tied a rock around his neck and threw him in a river instead.

Tom's grandmother had given him the medal on his first day as a fireman, and he'd worn it every day since. At the beginning of each shift, he'd take it from his locker and drop it over his head, then button a collared uniform shirt over it. He never wore the department-issued T-shirt. Too casual for an officer. Then he would pin his badge, number seventy-nine, to his breast pocket, where he always kept a pen and a small, spiral-bound notebook. That was one of the obvious differences: Tom looked like an officer because that's what he happened to be; Sully pinned his silver bars to his knit winter cap because that's what he wanted people to see. It rubbed a lot of guys the wrong way, like he was flaunting his smarts, reminding everyone that he tested higher than they did.

No matter. Tom had a soft spot for everybody. "The true sign of class," he used to tell his kids, "is the man who treats the homeless person and the president the same way." Or the young lieutenant the same as the chief.

He smiled at Sully. "Well, as long as you're ready," he said. "But don't get too excited."

He walked away chuckling. He was a little melancholy, expecting this was his last night on Ladder 2, but he was still in a jovial mood. After lunch with Kathy, he'd spent the afternoon mapping her walking tour through midtown Manhattan. It reminded him of all the places he liked in New York, how much he liked the city. And his regular crew was there for his final tour on the ladder. Good firemen, all three of them, veterans with six decades of experience between them. He'd miss working with them, but he wasn't going far; the Fire Prevention office was in the same building as the Grove Street station, which meant he'd see all the guys when they worked day tours.

To look at the men of Ladder 2, though, Tom appeared out of place, like the runt of the Ladder 2 litter. Paul Brosnihan, Paul Grazulis, and Tim Jackson were all giant men, beefy with the vaguely surly look of longshoremen, each at least six feet tall, towering over their lieutenant, the Lilliputian. He remembered his wife, Kathy, had been afraid of Tim Jackson the first time she met him, which was reasonable because Tim could be a scary-looking guy. He had sandy hair giving way to gray, a mustache that arched down past the corners of his mouth to his jaw, and arms that could bench two-fifty without breaking a sweat, three hundred if he grunted. There was a tattoo of the Harley-Davidson logo on one bicep and the insignia of the 101st Airborne, the Screaming Eagles, on the other. Tim had signed on to fight with them in Vietnam, damn near died with them, too, saw three of his buddies turn to crimson mist before his eyes, his own body blown backward by the concussion of a mortar shell, floating through the air, slow motion, his mind repeating over and over, *I'm not dead, I'm not dead, holy fuck, I'm not dead.* He still carried shrapnel in one arm and one leg.

Tim was the other reason Tom was in a good mood, the reason he was smiling to himself every so often. The lieutenant was planning a joke, had already gathered the supplies and planned the operation. Tom Spencer might not have been the funniest man in the station, perhaps not the quickest with the verbal jab or the sophomoric put-down. But he was the most elaborate, orchestrating pranks that required hours, sometimes days, of setup and delivery. At the moment, he had several dozen clear white Christmas bulbs, the ones the size of a man's thumb, stacked in his basement. One night the following week, when he knew Tim would be working, Tom planned on driving to Hopedale, a tiny and semirural bedroom community south of Worcester, where Tim lived in a pale yellow bungalow with his wife, Mary. On the front lawn was a blue spruce strung with blue lights rigged to a timer so they would automatically light at dusk. Tom was going to unscrew every blue bulb and replace it with a white one.

Tom thought that would be very funny. He wouldn't even

have to see Tim's face when the tree lit up white; just imagining it was good enough. Kathy, on the other hand, suspected that this was an inordinate amount of effort for a prank. "Oh, no," Tom had told her. "Just to know Timmy, to know how much he loves that tree. When he gives us directions, it's a landmark. 'When you see the blue lights on the tree, that's it.'" Then he laughed. Tonight, seeing Tim in the station, he tried to keep a straight face. It wasn't easy.

The spruce on Tim Jackson's front lawn was almost fifteen feet tall now, and almost as wide, a robust evergreen, round and fat and full. A second one stood next to it, farther back from the road, the two of them rising like a bushy, bluish screen to block out the traffic on Mendon Street.

He'd planted both of them himself. The larger one, the older one, was a sapling he'd brought home at Christmastime eleven years earlier, in 1988, the first Christmas after he married Mary. They decorated it with tiny ornaments and put it on the sun porch. Then, when the weather warmed, Tim scooped a hole from the half-thawed ground, nestled it into the soil so the roots could take hold and the branches could push up into the Hopedale sky. He called it God's Country, his patch of green on the edge of the village cemetery, and it seemed an appropriate thing to say because Tim Jackson finally felt blessed.

He was almost forty years old when he found Mary. He had left two wives in the past, along with a whole other life, a different, darker image of himself. He grew up on the wrong side of the tracks, which was the south side of the Boston and Albany line, in a dense neighborhood of wood-framed tenements stacked on steep hills and bordered on one side by Worcester Cold Storage and the rest of the stinking warehouses and on another by the county jail and the Worcester Asylum for the Hopelessly Insane. Every inch of it was eventually demolished, perhaps mercifully, to make room for the interstate and a housing project. His aunt and uncle raised him because his parents, an exceptionally fertile couple that drifted between Worcester and Providence, couldn't cope with all seventeen of their children. He wasn't an unhappy child, but he always wondered why his mother never came back for him.

He got his sweetheart pregnant about the same time he was finishing high school, married her, and then left her to go fight the Communists in Vietnam. He was a good soldier, earned his Purple Heart and his Bronze Star and a couple of other medals before limping back to Worcester in 1971. He never returned to his family life, though. Mostly, he found companionship in a bottle. He wasn't much of a husband, leaving for weeks at a time, stopping by to see his son every so often, nursing a cup of tea, waiting to leave. That marriage officially ended in early 1973, but it had essentially been over for almost six years. The second time around wasn't much better. He married a British expat named Lesley in 1976, fathered another son, then limped along for eight years before that union fell apart as well.

Tim was a good fireman, though, a great one, even. He had joined the department in 1972, sat through the same drill class as Mike McNamee, and quickly developed a reputation for fearlessness, as if he needed to taunt the flames, stare them down, prove he was tougher than fire. He had to be ordered out of a building more than once, sprinting, diving clear with orange tentacles lunging after his boots. He worked Rescue 1 for years, approached the job with a soldier's code: never leave a man behind. And he thrived on the action. "After Vietnam," he told his second wife, "where else could I find that kind of excitement?" Sometimes Lesley would confess that she was afraid for him, afraid she'd be left a widow. "Don't be afraid, honey," Tim would tell her. He always smiled when he said that, like he was secretly remembering the punch line to one of his long, opaque jokes. "Yes, every alarm could be the last alarm. But don't worry about it. If it is, they'll have one of those big funerals for me. Everyone'll come. It'll be great."

The booze proved to be more dangerous than the flames, almost cost him his career. Tim was never a fall-down drunk. Nasty sometimes, and occasionally belligerent, but always functional. But the brass didn't like smelling beer on his breath, didn't think it was a good idea for a man to be climbing on burning roofs and crawling through smoke-black rooms if his head wasn't completely clear. They warned him once, then twice. Tim decided he liked being a fireman more than he liked liquor.

That was 1984, after his second divorce. He met Mary Flynn the following year, watched her come through the door of a nightclub called the Driftwood, hips gently swaying under a too-tight white dress. He fell in love right then. She barely noticed him. She flirted with Tim's buddy Gary, asked him to dance during a ladies-choice number, took his business card when Gary asked for her number, disappeared out the door.

Tim saw her a week or so later, at a Halloween party. He had a rubber mask pulled over his head, a wrinkly latex face with a fringe of matted gray hair around the bald crown. A bolo tie was knotted around his neck, and he kept an overcoat pulled around his waist, flashing it open every so often to reveal fake pant legs held up with elastic around his knees and a pair of boxer shorts stuffed with a plastic baby rattle. A dirty old man. He waved at Mary across the floor, danced with her once or twice, and followed her outside when the party broke up.

"You don't remember me, do you?" he said.

Mary laughed. "No. How could I? I can't see your face."

"I'll take my mask off if you'll give me a kiss," Tim said.

Mary laughed again. She blushed.

"Really. I'll take it off if you'll give me a kiss."

Mary looked at him for a moment, considering, coy. "Okay," she said. "Take your mask off."

Tim tugged at the edge of the latex, lifted it up, peeled the old man away from his young man's face. He smiled, his mustache following the rise of his mouth.

Mary studied his features. He was familiar, but she couldn't quite place him.

"You don't remember me, do you? Because I remember you."

"Yes, of course I do . . ." She looked more closely, quiet, stalling for time. Then it came to her. "The Driftwood," she said, half triumphant, half relieved. "You were at the Driftwood that night."

"Yes!"

Mary examined him now, an exaggerated appraisal. "Yeah," she said slowly, "you're not too bad."

She kissed him on the cheek to hold up her end of the deal. Tim asked for her number, and she demurred again. But she offered to take his.

Then she made him wait. Two weeks after Halloween, she finally dialed his number. "Wow," Tim said when he heard her voice. "I'd just about given up on you."

A few days before Thanksgiving, he bought her dinner in the restaurant of the Sheraton Hotel in Milford, a small town southeast of Worcester. He was charming and considerate, a downright gentleman. Mary wasn't sure exactly what she was looking for in a man, but she'd been divorced long enough to have figured out what she didn't want. No cads, drunks, or playboys. Tim wasn't any of those things. In fact, one of the first things she noticed was how honest he was. On their fourth date, he told her about his years of drinking and his months of sobriety, the kind of red flag most men would be too wary to hoist. But as the months wore on, through the fifth date and the tenth and the fiftieth, the pieces fell into place. Tim was a walking twelve-step program. He wasn't preachy or pious about it, but humbled and introspective and serenely uncritical. He knew where the bottom was, knew anyone could plummet, dropping straight down and landing hard. "There but for the grace of God," he used to say whenever the conversation turned to a wino or a hobo or some other troubled soul. "There but for the grace of God go I."

For all that, they had a playful romance. Tim took Mary along on his second job, driving a charter bus—if a man can drive a fire truck, he can drive a bus—full of tourists to see the seaside mansions in Newport and the kaleidoscope hills of autumn leaves. In the warmer months, Tim would kick his motorcycle, a Triumph and, later, a Harley-Davidson, into gear, tell Mary to hold on tight behind him, and roar down a country two-lane, north into Vermont and New Hampshire and south to Connecticut, all across New England. When they came upon a roadside shop that sold country crafts or primitive gewgaws, Mary would flap her arms against his sides so Tim would know to pull over, which he always did. In the spring, they would ride all the way to Washington, D.C., for a motorcycle rally called Rolling Thunder, a horde of military veterans rumbling into the capital in honor of their comrades who went missing in action and the prisoners of war who never came home. Tim would ride straight to the Vietnam veterans memorial to pay his respects. He took a picture once of a panel into which had been etched with three soldiers named Jackson, all killed in the jungle. There, too, but for the grace of God.

Mary knew fairly early that she would marry Tim. But two bad marriages will make a man skittish. Tim was deliberate, cautious, drawing out the courtship until he was certain he'd sorted love from lust. And Mary was patient. More than two years after their first date, on St. Patrick's Day 1988, he asked her to be his wife.

"Let's just do it," he said. "No fanfare, nothing fancy. We've both had all that. Let's just do it."

Two weeks later, on Easter Sunday, they were married by a justice of the peace. They spent that night at a small inn in New Hampshire, stayed for a few honeymoon days, then moved into Mary's pale yellow Cape in Hopedale.

It was the first real house Tim had ever lived in, a home that wasn't stacked into a triple-decker or carved out of an old Victorian. He dug up the yard, planted Korean lilacs and white hydrangeas and climbing yellow roses and pink azaleas. He built a deck under a pergola outside the kitchen with a view of the cemetery and grafted an addition onto the side, next to the dining room, with a planked ceiling and a fieldstone fireplace and a wide window where he could sit in his armchair and watch his blue spruces grow. He kept his magazines and books in neat piles on either side of his chair, *Hog Tales* and *Cruising Rider* in a wicker basket to the left, *Essential Shrubs* and *Family Circle*'s gardening supplement on a small table to the right.

Winter was the worst time of year for Tim. He couldn't ride his bike, for one. And except for the evergreens, the yard was barren, nothing more than brittle sticks poking up through the muddy snow. He would count the weeks until spring, wait for the sun to warm the soil, for the buds of the hydrangeas to curl from the stalks. On the first fine day, he and Mary would sit on the deck, and Tim would draw in a deep breath, smell the greening on the breeze. "Well," he'd say, "we made it through another one." And Mary would smile at him and nod her head and they would raise their coffee cups to all that was blooming around them.

Lieutenant Sullivan stayed close to Engine 3, his attention focused on the radio. He heard the alert tones, shrill beeps cutting through the background noise, the roar of the fire and the splash of water and the muffled voices of men yelling to each other. He checked the time: 6:39. Then a dispatcher's voice, repeating Mike McNamee's order: "All companies working inside the structure, use extreme caution. There may be holes in the floor, building may be extremely unsafe. Once again, all companies in the interior use—"

The transmission was cut off. Another man pushing his talk button, stepping on dispatch.

Sully fiddled with his turnout coat, made sure the sleeves were straight, the clasps working. *Three alarms.* He could still smell it.

One minute passed.

"Car 2 to Fire Alarm." The deputy chief, Jack Fenton, one rank above McNamee.

"Fire Alarm answering Car 3." Man, it was hard to hear the words clearly, decipher the syllables, figure out who was talking and what he was saying.

"Give me a third alarm."

"Ten-four."

Sully was moving before the loudspeaker honked on the wall above the apparatus floor. "Let's go," he yelled to his men. Jay Lyons sprinted to the driver's side, moving more urgently, with more excitement, than he had for the one-tone medical run. Joe

McGuirk, Doug Armey, and Mark Fleming piled into the compartment behind the cab. Across the floor, Tom Spencer and his men clambored aboard Ladder 2.

Both engines growled as the garage doors rolled up. Thirty seconds after the alarm sounded, two more trucks rumbled into the night. A third truck, Engine 7, was screaming toward the warehouse from the other side of city.

12

MIKE MCNAMEE WAS IN THE STAIRWELL, ON THE LANDING outside the door to the third floor, when the third alarm was struck. He didn't make the call. The deputy chief, Jack Fenton, did. Anytime a fire went to two alarms, a deputy chief, one rank above a district chief like McNamee, was sent to the scene to assume full command. At that point, McNamee took over the interior command, which, since the battle against Worcester Cold Storage was being fought only inside, still left him essentially in charge.

He was relieved to hear the call for more men. The moments lost on the third floor, staring at identical doors, had rattled him. Fire Alarm hadn't found any information on the building, floor plans or lists of hazardous chemicals that might be stored inside. There was too much he didn't know about the building, too many odd corridors and dark caverns. His men had the fire corralled on the second floor, just beyond the firewall. Engines 1, 12, and 6 and Ladders 1 and 5 were attacking from the B side, and guys from Engines 13 and 16 had two hoses running up the C stairs. But they'd been at it for a while, almost twenty minutes in an oven. Fresh reserves wouldn't hurt. The third alarm would bring a dozen men on two engines and a ladder.

He looked around the stairwell, his eyes already adjusted to the shades of black and gray. The railing was a wide line of ink, ruler-straight, angling up against the charcoal walls. The spot from his flashlight caught certain shapes, threw shadows that bled into the gloom. The walls muffled the sounds of a firefight, the rough hiss of the flames, the dull thud of boots pounding on the steps below, the clank of tools banging against metal. He listened for a moment, alone on the stairs. Everything sounded normal. Every man was doing his job. *We can still get this,* he thought.

Mike turned toward the stairs, started to climb to the floor above. His boot found the first step with a rubbery thud. Mike raised his other foot, saw the metal tread of the stairs beneath him.

Then it was gone. In a heartbeat, the stairwell went black. His foot, the steps, the railing, his hand held less than an inch from his face—everything disappeared into a viscous cloud. The smoke had dropped from above, but in an instant, making it seem like it came from everywhere at once, as if every molecule of air had spontaneously alchemized into dark poison. There had been no warning, no bang or pop or rumble above the roar of the fire, just an immediate plunge into darkness.

Mike was caught off guard, his mask still clipped to his coat. The first breath seared his throat, and his eyes began to water, tears trying to wash away the sting. "I want everyone on the upper floors down to the ground now," he hollered up the stairs. "And I want head counts. I want everyone accounted for." He felt for the radio mike, squinting against the smoke, yelled the same order over the air, but missed the talk button. It never broadcast, but it didn't matter. From above, Mike could hear boots pounding down the stairs. His men would regroup on the first floor, adjust their attack.

He snapped his mask into place, drew in a gulp of fresh air. The smoke was still blinding, but the plastic kept it out of his eyes. He grabbed a railing in the dark and started down, banging his heels against the risers to find each step. Twenty-seven years on the job, and he'd never witnessed so awful a transformation, a building deteriorating that far that fast. He wondered if one of the upper floors had flashed, if hot gases had flooded rooms coated with cork and polystyrene, superheating the walls until they ignited. There was so much smoke, banking down so fast, pouring through hallways, into the stairwell, a force seeming to overwhelm physics, a boiling mist descending, collapsing, on the floors below.

It took Mike almost fifteen seconds to climb down three floors. The door on the ground floor was tucked behind a half wall, same as on the third floor, practically hidden. He'd remembered how many flights he'd gone up, knew where to break hard right to get out. In the foyer, just inside the loading dock, he pulled off his mask, coughed the smoke from his throat, gulped fresh air. He was bewildered, stunned, at how rapidly the stairwell had darkened, but he didn't dwell on it. No point and no time. The fire had made a tactical maneuver, ambushed him. Now he had to counter.

First he had to get the smoke out of the building, open more holes, give the cloud a way into the open sky. He went outside, looked up the side of the building. A series of arches were framed into one wall, old windows along the stairwell that had been covered with plywood. He grabbed his radio. "Command to Scope 2."

"Scope 2."

"Can you set up behind Engine 1, and underneath Ladder 1, and start taking these windows out on the side?"

"Received."

Mike glanced up the wall again. Those boards were meant

to seal the building tight. They wouldn't just pop open. His men would be working in a miasma of poison for at least ten more minutes. He keyed his microphone again. "Interior, Fire Alarm."

"Fire Alarm answering Interior."

"Notify the shop we're going to need some air at the scene."

"Interior, say again."

Damned radios. Even when no one stepped on the transmission, hit his talk button in the middle of someone else's sentence, or had his microphone short out when it got splashed with water, messages still got garbled. It required a practiced ear and steady concentration to decipher the words, separate them from the background noise. "We're going to need air," Mike said again. "Notify the shop, we are going to need resupply for our air."

"I have that."

Mike paced outside, studied the building, reconsidered everything he knew so far. There had been a report of homeless people living inside, but that had been twenty minutes ago, long enough for his men to search the building. They'd found evidence that someone was squatting there, the garbage and the waste, but no people. The tramps were out, had to be by now. The actual fire, meanwhile, was isolated but ferocious. Judging by the smoke, the density and the speed with which it had hemorrhaged into the stairs, the flames were exceptionally hot, generating more heat than could escape through the vent on the roof. And the building was dangerous, cagey. It had fooled Mike, confused him with its identical doors and twisting passages, even before it flooded black. Now his men were working blind, trying to feel their way through a furnace.

He considered ordering everyone out. His men could fall back into a defensive perimeter, line up the hoses, blast away from a safe distance—surround and drown. It wasn't glamorous, but it was effective, guaranteed a victory. Worcester firemen always won, too. The whole building might burn to the ground, but the fire always went out and everyone always went home.

Sirens whined in the middle distance, coming closer, louder with every whoop. The third-alarm companies. John Sullivan tried to raise Mike on the radio. No answer. Again. No answer. The third call caught Mike's attention, grabbed him through the chaos of the battle.

"Engine 3," he said into his radio. He could see the truck's lights flashing under the interstate. "Just hold tight there. Stage."

He wasn't sure where to send them yet. Another minute, maybe two, and he'd have to reposition all the men on the street.

The engines were pumping one thousand gallons a minute into the mass of flames just beyond the firewall. Robert A. watched it all disappear, swallowed into the orange, almost as if the fire was separating the droplets, feeding on the hydrogen and oxygen. "This is like pissing into a furnace," he muttered to himself.

Lt. Robin Huard from Engine 12 was next to him, manning a two-and-a-half-inch. Robin was fifty-three, but tougher than most guys half his age. Pumped iron for two hours every day. After almost twenty years on the job, he'd gotten hurt only once, when the harness of his air tank snagged on a latch in the truck. He tried yanking it free, but the harness was stronger than the ligaments holding his arm into the socket.

Engine 12 had responded on the first alarm. Eighteen minutes later, at 6:31, Robin was dragging hose up to the second floor. He ran into Bobby Mansfield, a ladder man out of the same station, coming down the stairs. Bob had been part of the initial crews on the roof, watched Paul Brotherton and Jerry

Lucey clean out the skylight. With the job on the roof accomplished, he moved downstairs with the rest of the men. The two guys from Rescue 1, Paul and Jerry, had turned into the top floor to check for the homeless people and any extension of the fire. Everyone else went lower to help with the attack.

Bobby and Robin got the line into position and, at 6:33, Robin radioed the order for his man on the truck to charge the line, arm them against the squalling flames. That was his favorite part, going into combat. And that's what it was, too, combat. He'd fought the Viet Cong thirty years earlier, 101st Airborne, a Screaming Eagle, drafted into the same branch of the army that Tim Jackson had signed on with. The principle had been the same: the enemy wanted to take his territory, kill him if they had to, and he wanted to take out the enemy. It was exhilarating. Danger was funny that way. Except Hamburger Hill, eight endless days neck deep in mud, dodging shrapnel and mortar shells. He'd never needed eight days to defeat a fire.

The first foray into the flames on the second floor went well, the leading flank collapsing as soon as they hit it. The small room they were in blacked out. Usually, that means the fire has been cooled, orange light replaced by smoke. But they could still hear the popping and snapping of a roaring blaze.

"Robin, this ain't right," Bobby said. "Can you hear it?"

"Yeah. And it's got heat," Robin said. "I can feel it on my neck." He paused. "Something's not right here. Something's going on that I don't understand."

He thought of Tina. They'd been married twenty-five years, raised two kids, built a big house on a lake just outside of town, filled it with antiques he collected. Tina was a nurse, tacked scraps of paper to the kitchen wall with affirmations printed on them, like "Pain is inevitable. Suffering is negotiable." She knew he was smart, careful, competent. Still, she would remind him sometimes: "Don't be a hero."

He and Bobby kept washing the walls, studying the room. The smoke was thickening, banking down. Air was rushing into the fire, hot gusts biting into his neck. It felt like wind. That wasn't good. Robin realized he'd lost track of time, that he'd lost his bearings. That was worse. He reassessed the battle. "There are no windows," he told himself. "You don't know where the staircase is, and you don't know how much air you have left." He felt a shudder of fear. "You're gonna get trapped in here. You're gonna die in here. You gotta get out."

Robin leaned close to Bobby, who was on the nozzle. "Drop the line," he yelled. "We're outta here."

Bobby kept spraying. Firemen were reluctant to retreat, back down from the enemy. "Drop the line," Robin hollered again.

Bobby took a step backward but kept the nozzle open.

"Drop the fucking line!" Robin screamed at him. "We're getting outta here, now."

Bobby slammed the valve shut, let the hose fall to the floor, turned for the doorway, following the hose back out. Robin was behind him. Something caught his leg, wrapped around it, pulled him down. The wires that had fallen from the ceiling. Another wave of smoke banked down, darkening Robin's vision. He clawed at the wires, knew he was running out of time.

A pair of hands broke through the clouds. Steve Adams, one of the men working his truck that night, was on his knees, next to the lieutenant, pulling away the wires. He got Robin untangled. Robin rolled onto his knees, found the hose on the floor, and started to crawl.

"No, it's this way," Steve yelled over the roar. He was pointing into a black maw.

Robin looked at him, unsure what to do. "Steve," he said, trying to steady his breathing, "you gotta be positive. You gotta be absolutely positive or we're gonna get lost in here."

"I'm positive," Steve said. "It's twenty-five feet, right there."

Robin took a deep breath, nodded. He stayed close to Steve, the two of them moving as fast as their knees would scrape against the floor. Twenty-five feet seemed like a mile. But then they were out on the stairs on the C side. Steve scrambled down. Robin turned around, went back into the darkness. He went to the edge of the vestibule, his radio in one hand, his thumb on the talk button. "Engine 12 to any firefighters in the second-floor area. Get out to the staircase, get out to the staircase." He released the button and screamed, "This way out! It's this way!" He didn't know if anyone heard him, if anyone was still floundering in the dark.

His mask vibrated against his face, a soft jackhammer warning him he was running out of air. He yelled once more, then wheeled around, hustling back to the stairs. He got to his feet, rushing now, hitting the treads on instinct, not bothering to feel for them. The fire growled behind him, his pulse pounded in his skull, his breath rasped behind the mask, all of it churning into a chaotic roar.

The mask cleaved to Robin's face as his boot hit the bottom step. He'd drawn the last breath, emptied the tank. It sucked back, like a vacuum pulling on his lungs. He never broke stride as he reached for the mask, ripped it off, gasping acrid air and sprinting outside.

Sixty feet above the pavement where Robin was wheezing, Jerry Lucey felt for his radio in the darkness. "Rescue 600 to Command," he said. "We need help. On the floor below the top floor of the building. We're lost."

No one answered. Paul Brotherton was next to him, the two of them on their hands and knees, keeping low, trying to get beneath the smoke. It was impossible. Everything was greasy black. They couldn't see each other, let alone the way out. Jerry wasn't too worried, though, not yet. He'd been here before, lost in a cauldron, wondering if he'd get to fresh air. He always did. Like that time in a triple-decker, the whole back end shrouded by a sheet of fire, Jerry looking for the stairs, going the wrong way, walking into the flames. One of the local sparkies took a picture of him from below, Jerry nothing more than a smudge in a wash of orange. He framed the picture, hung it in his basement rec room next to the Gottleib Rescue 911 pinball machine and above the stuffed dalmatian and opposite the *Backdraft* poster. Hell of a movie, *Backdraft.* Jerry had watched it more times than he could count. But Hollywood could never get the fire scenes right. In the movies, a burning warehouse was all orange light and bright flashes. "That is so fake," he'd tell Michelle. "If they really showed what it was like, the screen would be black."

If only he had a rope. Jerry thought every man, especially rescue guys, should carry a length of fireproof rope, a leader he could tie off where he came in, mark his trail. His would have been knotted to the door by the B stairwell, all the way across the warehouse. After they left the roof, he and Paul had swept the top level. From the top of the stairs, they moved quickly through two storerooms off the vestibule, then went into the main chamber. It was the same as on the lower floors: eighty-eight feet wide and fifty feet deep, bounded on the far end by a brick fire wall. They passed through that into a slightly smaller room, then turned left toward the C-side elevator shaft. They were able to get around the smoke and embers blowing up toward the vent, move around to the back side of the shaft, explore the whole floor. They saw nothing that alarmed them.

With the top floor clear, they backtracked to the stairs on the B wall. They had no choice: the stairwell next to the C elevator, the one Robin Huard had escaped through, went only to the third floor. Above that level, there was only one way up or down.

Jerry concentrated on his breathing, kept it slow, measured. The temperature was rising, 200 degrees, maybe 220. Heat expanded the air in his tank, made it seem thinner, made each breath seem shallow. If a man wasn't careful, he'd pant through the last few pounds in short, gasping moments. He retraced their path again in his head. They'd taken roughly the same route as they had on the floor above: across the chamber, through the fire wall, around one room, left through the elevator shaft. They were in the back corner, behind the shaft, when the lights went out. All that smoke, pouring in from everywhere at once. It smothered everything, even the beams from their flashlights. He and Paul had tried following the walls, feeling a path back out to the stairs, but they'd only gone in circles. Above him, chest-high if he'd been standing, Jerry could feel a narrow ledge, like the sill of a window. But he couldn't put his hand through it.

Paul's alarm went off, his mask rattling against his face. He had three minutes of air left, four if he was lucky. Fifty-five seconds had passed since Jerry had called for help, and still no answer. They could hear Jack Fenton, the deputy chief, calling the third-alarm companies, telling them to get to the second floor, relieve the men on the hoses. Jerry's transmission must have gotten lost in the chatter and the static.

He keyed the microphone again. "Rescue to Command, Rescue to Command." He measured each word, not wasting oxygen. "We need help on the fourth floor, one floor down. We're running out of air."

Fifteen seconds ticked by. Then Mike McNamee's voice. "Last message, can you repeat? Last message?"

Other voices clicked on immediately after Mike, jamming

the airwaves. Robert A.: "Engine 1 to Command, get everybody out of the second floor, back them out." Jack Fenton: "Command to Fire Alarm." Fire Alarm answering. Twenty-two more seconds gone.

Paul pushed his talk button. "Fire Alarm, Fire Alarm. Emergency, emergency! Clear the air, clear the air! Emergency!"

On the floors below them, dozens of men felt a spasm of dread. What they heard, what they would later swear they heard, was, "Mayday, mayday." Perhaps the syllables had been distorted by the background noise and the sketchy frequency. Or maybe it was Paul's tone, urgent and almost bewildered, and every other man's nerves that twisted one word into the other. Whatever the reason, they would remember it, be haunted by it, because they knew how frightened Paul must have been. Firemen were loath to speak that word, "mayday," ashamed to call for help, to admit that the heat and the smoke and the flames might be tougher than they were. Men called mayday only before they died, or when they believed they would.

Two more broadcasts followed in quick succession. First Jerry. "I have an emergency." Then Paul. "Command, we are two floors down from the roof," he said. "This is the Rescue company. Come now, come now."

The transmissions were breaking up, chopped by fragments of static and the background drone of the fire. "Okay," Mike answered. "Where are you? Where are you?"

"Two floors down from the roof."

He got on the radio. "All companies, we have an emergency. Somebody is two floors down from the roof."

"Guys, we're . . ." A different voice. Jerry. "Not the top floor. One floor down."

Mike broadcast again. "What is your emergency?"

Fire Alarm answered, clear and distinct, so every man could hear it. "Running out of air."

"Command to Engine 3."

Lt. John Sullivan heard Mike McNamee call his truck. He punched his radio. "Engine 3."

"Come up to the side of the building," Mike told him. He kept the message short, clipped, not wasting time or breath. Mike had blocked out all emotion, distilled the operation to a tactical chore. He had two men—*his* men—lost in the black mist above, frightened and choking and probably dying. Mike couldn't afford to be afraid. No one below the fifth floor could.

Sully didn't bother answering, just started moving. Instinct took over. There wasn't much in the manuals about moments like this, two men missing. There didn't have to be: when one man is in trouble, every other man goes after him.

He called back over his shoulder, "Jay, shut it down. You're coming in. You take Joe. I'll take Mark and Doug."

Jay Lyons nodded, jumped down from the cab. At most fires, the driver usually stayed with the truck, ran the pumps and fed the lines. He was also the only man not fully dressed for battle; a man couldn't drive a firetruck very well if he'd had a tank of air strapped to his back. Jay reached for a harness, slipped his shoulders through it, shrugged, rolled the air bottle into postion between his shoulder blades.

Joe McGuirk watched Sully and the others run toward the warehouse while Jay put on his gear. He was eager, excited, desperate to get inside. Joe had never been in a big one before, never seen enough fire for everyone. The worst danger Joe had faced on the job was a medical run when an overdosed junkie puked all over him, splashed vomit in his eyes. He had to worry for a couple weeks that he might have been infected with hepatitis. Nothing heroic about that. This is what he'd waited for, the mission that was born into him, the stuff of lore and legend. He was a real fireman going to save real lives, his brothers' lives.

He was relieved Sully had left him with Jay. Of the two, Joe would probably see more action with Jay. He always wondered if Sully was too timid. Those times Sully had let slower trucks overtake Engine 3, let other men jump into the flames—sure, it was protocol, Engine 3 taking its assigned spot as second due. Joe understood that. But he still suspected that maybe Sully wasn't as eager to jump into the flames as some of the other guys. Guys like Jay. Jay was aggressive, a warrior. "Ballsy," like Sully said. Joe wanted to be ballsy, too. Once Jay made lieutenant, maybe he'd get assigned to a ladder truck, and maybe he'd take Joe with him. Joe hoped he would.

Jay fastened the clasps on his coat, double-checked his harness, made sure his mask was clipped to his shoulder. He felt for his medallion, St. Florian on a silver chain around his neck, similar to Tom Spencer's. Around the saint's image were four words stamped in relief: SAINT FLORIAN. PROTECT US.

Jay looked at Joe. He saw Joe's jaw set firm, his teeth clenched. But there was a shine to his eyes. "You ready?" he asked Joe.

Joe nodded. He realized he wasn't afraid. "Let's do it."

The two of them broke into a light jog, the warehouse looming above them, rising with perspective until it overtook everything, filled their entire vision, a smoking hulk splashed with the red and white of the firetrucks' lights.

Mike shook off the fear that stirred in his belly. Paul had called mayday. He was sure of it, and he was terrified by it, or would have been if he dwelled on it. He couldn't afford that. Paul and Jerry couldn't afford that.

Finding them would be impossible if Mike couldn't figure out where they were, at least which floor. Paul had said two down from the roof, but that wouldn't do the men starting to search from the bottom much good if they didn't know how many levels the warehouse had. Mike sprinted outside, faced the building, craned his neck toward the sky. He studied the facade, pored over it for a clue—a break in the pattern of bricks, the weathered arch of an old window, anything that might tell him where Paul and Jerry were lost. He checked one wall, darted around the back, then back to the front. Nothing. Worcester Cold Storage wasn't giving up any of its secrets.

Mike hurried back to the stairs at the same time the third-alarm companies were storming the building. He decided to post himself in the stairwell so he could keep track of everyone, who went up and who came safely down. He saw John Sullivan coming with two of his men. "Sully, we need more bottles," he said. "Can you get us more air?"

Sully and his men went back outside, onto Arctic Street, to find a truck with a spare stash of air tanks. As they left, Tom Spencer and two of his men, Tim Jackson and Paul Brosnihan, clambered over the loading dock and into the foyer. Mike noticed the look at Tim's face, which was unusual because it betrayed nothing. No fear, no anxiety. Just a quiet determination, the countenance of a man who accepted that he signed on for a job that might actually require him to get hurt. Mike thought Tim must have been a hell of a soldier.

He turned to Lieutenant Spencer. "All right, Tommy, I need you to go to the fifth floor," he said. "Stay on the ropes, stay together, and leave before your low-air alarm goes off."

Tom nodded as he tightened his mask around his face. Mike caught his eyes, looked hard into them for a moment. Three curious facts flashed through his mind. *Patrick, Casey, Daniel.* Tom's kids. He knew all their names, how old they were. He was sending their father into a poisoned void.

Tom held the gaze, but only for an instant. His mask secure, he brushed by Mike and disappeared into the cloud, Brosnihan and Tim following hard behind him.

He heard Dave Halvorsen, Rescue 1's lieutenant, on the radio. "Rescue to Paul Brotherton." A pause. "Rescue 1 to Rescue 600."

"Yeah, go ahead," Paul said. "Go ahead."

"Six hundred, what's your location?" Dave was cool, almost formal, using Paul's call sign.

"Two floors down from the roof. Two floors down from the roof. Please hurry."

Paul was pleading. Time was burning away.

"Rescue to Rescue 600."

"Go, yeah." It was Jerry again. They were taking turns on the radio. Dave didn't recognize the voice, couldn't tell it was a different man.

"You all right, Paul? You all set?"

"We need air, we need air. We're sharing a tank right now, off of me."

"Paul, if you need air, come on down. Come down."

Paul answered next, gave the mask to Jerry. "We're lost, Dave," he said. "You gotta send a rescue team up here for us." He sounded perplexed. Not desperate yet, but confused, baffled.

"What floor?" Dave asked. "What floor?"

"Second floor down from the roof. Two floors down, I think."

Jerry gave the tank to Paul, barked into his own radio. "We were on the roof, and then we checked the next floor down," he said. "Now we are on the next one. Hurry." Forty seconds later, he pushed the talk button again. "Get up here. Please."

It was 6:52. Paul and Jerry had been lost for at least six minutes—longer, probably, considering Jerry broadcast their initial call for help at 6:46. One air tank was already drained, and the second couldn't have more than another handful of breaths left in it. After that, they would be forced to pull the mask away or die gasping. Once it was off, though, the only thing left to breathe would be smoke, a venomous mix of carbon monoxide and, depending on what was burning, several hundred or several thousand toxic chemicals. Hydrogen cyanide and hydrochloric acid were probably in the vapor. And the asphalt and polystyrene on the walls were the industrial equivalent of napalm, petroleum by-products superheated into a poison mist.

They were already woozy from the carbon monoxide, maybe already crippled, their muscles paralyzed. A heavy concentration reduced a man to a paralytic stupor in five breaths, the CO bonding to the red blood cells, starving the body of oxygen. The brain, trying to save itself, would shut down the least important tissues, everything except itself, the heart, and the lungs. That's why firemen were always finding civilians unconscious next to doors and windows, overwhelmed by carbon monoxide one desperate lunge from safety.

While the CO was shutting down their bodies, the other toxins were destroying their airways. The smoke particles would have irritated their bronchial tubes and lung tissues at room temperature. Superheated, they scorched the deepest parts of Paul's and Jerry's chests, burning all the way into the tiniest air sacs. Their throats were closing, swelling shut from the trauma, the same way a finger swelled if it was slammed in a door. But there wouldn't be much pain. The CO would knock them out before it hurt too badly.

Jack Fenton struck a fourth alarm immediately after Jerry's transmission. Two more engines, one more ladder, nine more men. Mike had three teams working up the stairs, three at the bottom waiting to take their place. Then another message from Paul, frantic now.

"Fire Alarm, we have a second emergency here," he said. "Get people up on this floor now or we are going to die. We have no air, and we cannot breathe."

"What floor are you on?" Fire Alarm radioed back. "What floor are you on?"

"We don't know," Paul said, his voice weaker now. "We don't know. We were on a wall. We have no air. Please."

13

WHEN THE SECOND FLOOR WENT BAD, THE FLAMES NEARLY exploding and the smoke instantly shrouding everything in oily vapor, Capt. Mike Coakley headed for the roof. It was a calculated risk. He knew going up meant fighting his way through the worst of the cloud, all that gas and dirty molecules rising on their own heat. But he also knew Worcester Cold Storage better than most men on the job. He'd been in it a number of times for routine inspections, always in the light, never under pressure. And he'd gotten lost. Like every other Worcester fireman, Coakley used to tell himself, *God, if that goes up, I hope I'm off duty.* So much for hoping. He remembered the door from the stairs to the ground floor was tucked behind a short wall, that he could stumble past it, find himself at a dead end in the basement, maybe get lost in a maze down there. Moving the other way was a straight run to the open night sky and relatively fresh air. There was an escape route waiting, too, Ladder 1's big aluminum stick rising up from the back of the truck. All things considered, up was a safer bet than down.

Bert Davis, one of his men from Ladder 1, followed him, the two of them humping double-time through the darkness. Immediately before the bulkhead at the roof, Bert felt a sharp whack against the top of his forehead: a metal pipe, hung low across the stairwell. He blinked the stars out of his eyes, ducked, bounded up into clear air.

Neither man liked the view from the top. The vent just beyond the fire wall, the skylight Paul and Jerry had smashed out, was a volcano, orange flames shooting up through it, blowing thirty feet into the air, embers spinning away like bottle rockets, smoke braided through the strands of fire. Closer to them, the roof was bubbling, the tar starting to melt, to boil. There was too much heat below, so much that it couldn't all escape through the huge hole Paul and Jerry had bashed out above the elevator shaft, 15 feet to a side, 225 feet square. The warehouse had become an enormous blast furnace: the flames on the second floor were drawing great drafts of oxygen through the loading dock doors, gorging on air, then exhaling through the elevator shaft, which was functioning as a massive chimney. Attacking the fire—by the numbers, a textbook operation—appeared to have only antagonized it. It was as if the building had set a booby-trap, lured the men in, then erupted.

Then Coakley felt a chill, despite the sizzling atmosphere. Paul on the radio. *We're lost, Dave. You gotta send a rescue team up here for us.* Coakley shuddered, felt his sweat go clammy. He knew Paul and Jerry were in peril, could hear it in their voices. He also knew where they were, give or take a couple dozen yards. Fifteen minutes earlier, after the roof had been vented and the hoses were positioned around the flames, Coakley had stood with Paul and Jerry on the fifth-floor landing. Coakley and Bert were going to help man the hoses. "You want to come down?" he'd asked the rescue guys. "Nah," Paul told him. "We'll finish this floor. Then we'll be down."

He heard Paul again. *Second floor down from the roof. Two floors down, I think.*

That meant they'd never finished the fifth floor. Coakley considered how much time had passed, mapped the building in his head from memory. Best guess, they'd crossed through the fire wall, had found the single opening between the two halves of the warehouse, then gotten turned around in the labyrinth on the far side. In clear light, it might take a man two minutes to cover that same ground, find them, get them a fresh bottle of air. Groping through a coal-black cloud on all fours would take five minutes, and then only if a man was guided by blind luck. Realistically, it was far longer, if it was even possible.

Coakley did more math. Paul and Jerry had one tank between them, buddy-breathing their last precious wisps of air. Their lives were being measured in minutes. How many? Two? Four? The exact number didn't matter; Paul and Jerry would be dead before anyone got to them. Coakley was sure of that. They could be recovered, but not rescued.

He leveled his stare at Bert, locked eyes with him. A Bible verse crept into his thoughts, something from Matthew. It was hard to remember. No, John. Definitely John, chapter 15. "A greater love hath no man than to lay down his life for his brothers." Something like that. It had been a noble abstract in Sunday school. On the roof, in the steam and the soot and the ferocious crackling, it was an obligation. Paul had been in the first drill class Coakley had taught, and one of the things he was supposed to have learned, that Paul did learn, was to never leave a man stranded.

"We gotta go get 'em," he told Bert. "Let's go."

It was an order. Bert didn't hear it as one, because Bert didn't need to be told to go save his friends. But Coakley meant it as one, an officer telling a subordinate what to do, relieving Bert of accountability. It was easier that way. In his mind, Coakley assumed responsibility for Bert's life.

Bert nodded, the quick, firm tilt of the chin that men do when they are very serious. They went back to the bulkhead, snapped their masks into place, and stepped into the darkness. They felt their way down one set of stairs, then a second flight. Coakley felt for the door into the fifth floor, pushed it open, then dropped to his knees. Bert was immediately behind him, one gloved hand holding tight to Coakley's coat.

They crawled inside the fifth floor, trying to move in a straight line, aiming for the fire wall on the far side. Coakley felt for a wall, something to keep his bearings. His air tank had already been tapped, part of it already inhaled. They'd have only about ten minutes inside, and only if they controlled their breathing, kept it steady.

Coakley felt something solid to his right. He swept his hand up, then down, moved it in a wide circle. A wall. He scooted forward, keeping in contact with the flat surface on his right. After a minute or so, he came to an inside corner. He shuffled left, keeping the wall to his right. More crawling. Another corner. Then a third and a fourth. Coakley's throat tightened. *I'm in a fucking room.* But he hadn't felt a door. A four-sided room had to have a door. They'd gotten in. There had to be a way out.

He kept moving, his knees scraping faster over the same stretch of warehouse floor he'd been around once. Four more corners. Coakley shifted his arm higher, up where the door handles should be. He remembered the iron rings lay flush, nestled in pockets, but maybe he could feel one in the dark.

Four more corners. Still no door. His heart raced. "Bert," he yelled over his shoulder, "we're going to die in here." He crawled forward, quelled the panic rising inside. He said the same words to himself, believed them. *I'm going to fucking die. I'm going to die for a piece of shit building, trying to save a guy who's already dead. I'm going to fucking die in here.* Logic took him the next step. *I've killed Bert. I've fucking killed Bert.*

His low-air alarm hadn't gone off yet. There was still time. He'd given Bert an order. Forget laying down his own life. His duty, his immediate and only obligation, was to get his man out alive. Behind him, Bert was thinking the same thing: he had to save his captain. They had to save each other.

They kept moving, knowing that to stop was to concede defeat, surrender to the building. Coakley focused on the time. How long had they been in there? He wasn't sure. His air had to be running low.

He swept his hand forward along the wall. His fingers jabbed a hard ridge. He reached for it with both gloves, slid all ten fingers against it. He felt a thin lip of metal. The door. A draft, a gust of heat or a hard puff of smoke, must have nudged it, pushed it in just far enough to be felt by a blind man. His heart pounded harder, two beats, three beats, twelve. Coakley rose up on his knees and pulled open the door, felt to make sure Bert was still with him, then edged through it. He paused, listened. The sounds—clomping boots, whining saws, clanking tools—were louder to the left. He turned, scuttled as quickly as his knees would move, felt another door, then the steel treads of the stairs. With Bert still behind him, he bolted down the stairs, his mask buzzing against his face as he cleared the final steps.

Bob Mansfield followed Robert A. up the stairs from the ground floor a minute after Paul's call for help. Both of them had a fresh bottle of air, but neither trusted the supply to hold out. They were breathing hard from hiking through black steam, kicking the risers of each step to find their way to the fourth floor.

They dropped to their knees and began to crawl. They didn't know if they were on the right floor, if they were crawling toward Paul and Jerry or beneath them. But maybe Paul and

Jerry didn't know precisely where they were, either. Other men were already searching the fifth floor. If there was a chance Paul and Jerry had made it down to the fourth, Robert A. and Bob weren't going to risk leaving them there.

The heat was ferocious, roiling the smoke, making it seem like the atmosphere was alive, angry, a predator smothering its prey. It wrapped around their masks, obliterated their vision, took away shadow and light. But they could feel it, moving with an unnatural velocity, swirls and eddies twisting around their arms and legs and chests as they inched forward, a physical presence that pushed back, pressed on them. And they could feel each other, Bob on Robert A.'s right shoulder, maintaining contact with one hand, holding a Haligan in the other. Robert A. had the only radio between them, and the background noise overwhelmed their voices unless they yelled in each other's ears. If they lost touch for more than a moment, they would lose each other.

It was difficult to know how far they'd gone, but Bob memorized the turns. He'd practiced how to maintain his bearings in utter darkness on the underwater rescue team. In a blackwater dive, men floated blind, losing sensory perception in three dimensions, side to side and front to back and up and down. At least in a fire he didn't have to worry about up and down, only the level movements. So far, he and Robert A. had made three lefts, tracing a giant U-shaped path into the warehouse. That's what it seemed like, anyway. Were they in fifty feet? One hundred? And how much air did they have left? It was impossible to be certain.

Robert A. wasn't taking chances. With two lives on the line, he wouldn't help anyone by getting himself lost. "We're far enough in," he said after the third left. "Let's get out of here. Because if we don't get out now, we're not getting out."

"All right," Bob said. He was relieved. The danger, the very real risk of dying, was outweighing the possiblity of finding Paul and Jerry on the fourth floor.

He felt Robert A. scoot forward and to the right.

"Hey, hey! Wrong way," he screamed. "You're going the wrong way. It's this way." He tugged Robert A.'s sleeve to the back and right, the reverse of the turns Bob remembered making.

"No, it's not," Robert A. shouted back. "It's this way."

He scooted forward again. Bob's hand slipped away. He reached for Robert A., felt nothing but smoke. Just a few feet away, Robert A. was groping for Bob. He turned for him, reached again. Nothing. They were both spinning, swinging their hands, desperate to reconnect. They called for each other, but the noise, the rush of hot air and the grumble of flames, washed away their voices, grabbed them in the short gap between the two men, carried them away.

Bob froze. His mind raced, two instincts, survival and duty, colliding, spinning around each other. Firemen didn't leave anyone alone in an inferno. Men lived because other men never left them alone to die. He couldn't leave Robert A., but he couldn't find him, either. Maybe Robert A. had switched directions, moved back the way Bob told him to go. Or maybe he'd crawled farther into the warehouse, made another turn, snaked into a corner. Bob didn't know, couldn't know. If he went after him, he'd just be guessing. And it would probably kill him.

He decided not to die. If he got out, got more air, he could come back. He could tell other men where to look, get someone to raise Robert A. on his radio, talk him back to the door. Nausea churned in his stomach as he lurched back and to the right, the way he remembered.

Bob crawled a few feet, then made the first right turn. He felt something hard and solid rise up in front of him. A wall. He spread out his hands, reached ahead. Another wall, coming into the first and forming a corner. "Shit," he whispered. He didn't remember any corners. It must be a room, he thought. But he shouldn't be in it, didn't know how he'd gotten there. He realized he'd made a mistake, maybe a fatal one.

Panic tickled his brain stem. He squeezed his eyes shut, shook his head, concentrated, forced his nerves to steady themselves. He'd been through this before, thinking he would die, trapped in a flaming cellar, three minutes of air in his tank, the hose that led out through a maze of boxes and shelves hidden under rubble and water. He'd panicked then, started to hyperventilate, convinced he didn't have enough oxygen to escape. "You dumb shit," he'd muttered next. "You keep breathing like that and you're definitely not getting out." Self-control had saved his life. This was the same thing, only worse.

He stopped moving, stayed in one spot, listening, hoping to key in on a sound that would lead him out. For a long moment, there was only the snarl of the fire. But then a sputter, the rapid *pop-pop-pop* of an engine jerking to life. He recognized it as a K-12, a heavy-duty saw that can tear through most anything. There had to be a fireman holding it. That had to be the way out.

Bob crawled toward the sound, feeling the wall as he went. Above him, he felt a small hole, just big enough to stick his head through. He stood up and peered into the black. The smoke seemed thinner, still black and oily but not quite as dense, breaking and fading in random places. A light shone through, disappeared behind another puff, reappeared. A searchlight, attached to one of the big aerial scopes. It had to be coming through one of the stairwell windows.

Safety was only a dozen yards away. He scurried along the wall, felt another corner, turned right. His hand hit a short ledge. A step, the step to the landing. He lurched to his feet, swept his leg forward, his brain telling his body to run, sprint to the ground, to fresh air.

He froze again. He couldn't leave. He'd been less wrong than Robert A., probably, anyway. If the captain was still inside, Bob had to get him out. He took a step back into the fourth floor, followed the wall until he came to a metal door. Then he swung at it with the Haligan, hit the steel as hard as he could. Once, twice, three times, big booms that rolled into the smoke. He stopped, listened.

"Keep doing that!" It was Robert A.'s voice, faint and muffled, but not far. Then it came again, louder, as if the captain had pulled off his mask, removed one barrier between his mouth and Bob's ears. "Keep doing that!"

Bob swung again, the Haligan light in his hands, adrenaline stoking his muscles and fear pumping out more adrenaline. He kept a steady beat, his pounding heart doubling for a metronome. The smoke rushed past him, a violent upward draft. He stood alone in the dark, banging and hoping for a minute or maybe three, each one dragging on for an hour. He felt something brush against his leg. Then Robert A. was on his feet, reaching for him, pushing at him, urging him down the stairs.

Mike McNamee paced at the bottom of the stairwell. Two minutes had passed since Paul Brotherton's last transmission. He'd never heard a man sound so desperate, never expected that when he did it would be Paul. *We have no air. Please.*

Mike keyed his radio. He had to raise Paul and Jerry, convince himself they were still alive, that they could still be found. He remembered their alarms, wondered if they'd sounded. Every fireman carried a small device attached to his coat called a PASS alarm, which stood for "Personal Alert Safety System." If a man remained motionless for thirty seconds, either overcome by smoke or trapped by debris, the alarm automatically sounded a piercing tone. There was also a panic button that could be pushed at will, setting off an auditory beacon for rescuers to home in on.

"Paul Brotherton, Rescue 1," Mike barked into his radio. "Paul Brotherton, activate your PASS system, activate your PASS system so we can hear you, activate your emergency alarm."

No answer. Mike ran outside, scanned the building again, desperate for a hint, anything. A minute passed before he heard his call sign on the radio.

"Command to Chief McNamee." It was Jack Fenton, the deputy chief. "Have you got the location of the men?"

"We have Ladder 1, Ladder 2, and Engine 3 looking," Mike answered.

Another thirty seconds ticked by. Still no answer from Paul or Jerry. Mike punched his talk button again. "Command to Paul Brotherton. Command to Jerry Lucey. Activate your PASS emergency."

Jerry answered, "They are activated."

Thank God, Mike thought. He had Coakley and his men on the roof, and Tom Spencer, Sully, and their men working their way up the stairs. "Ladder 1, Ladder 2, Engine 3," he said into his microphone. "They have activated their PASS alarms up there."

Maybe they'd caught a break. The sound of a PASS alarm could penetrate lead-dense smoke, cut through blackness that smothered the brightest lights, reflected all the photons back upon themselves. If his men could hear Paul and Jerry, Mike knew, they could crawl to them, get a fresh tank snapped onto their masks, bring them out alive.

The actual fire, raging on the second floor, was still basically contained. It was worsening, growing more vicious with each passing minute, but it hadn't spread much beyond the old office area. And a fourth alarm had been struck three minutes earlier. Two more engines and a ladder were only blocks away.

They were all undermanned, only three men on each truck, but any fresh set of legs and lungs would help.

For the next two minutes, Mike counted heads, coordinated men with positions, made sure everyone was accounted for. Tom Spencer and Tim Jackson were on the fifth floor, Sully was working his way up to the fourth floor. He had four good pairs of ears listening for Paul and Jerry. There was still time, though precious little of it.

At 6:57, he heard Sully's voice on the radio. Mike had sent him up to the third floor with Mark Fleming. From the doorway, down on his belly, Sully could see into the warehouse beneath a bank of smoke that hung a foot above the floor. He'd crept in, Mark trailing him, both of them lugging extra air tanks for Paul and Jerry. Conditions worsened by the minute, the smoke dropping, heat rising. They pressed into the miasma, inching all the way to the firewall on the far side. "They're not in here," he told Mark. "We gotta go up." They found their way back to the stairwell and started climbing, pausing on the landings of each floor to listen for the squeal of an alarm.

"Engine 3 to Command," Sully said. "Engine 3 to Command."

Jack Fenton answered. "Command."

"Chief, we made it all the way to the top, and we hear no alarms on this side of the building."

"Engine 3, if you can't reach them"—a burst of static—"get the hell out of there."

Mike's stomach turned to lead. Paul and Jerry must have been buried somewhere deep inside, behind the walls layered with cork and polystyrene, materials thick enough to mute the whine of their PASS alarms. He stopped tracking time—the heat of a firefight melts seconds into minutes and minutes into seconds, all of it lost in a blur—but he knew he was running out of it. He returned to the base of the stairs, watching his men, keeping track of them. A PASS alarm for Engine 6 sounded, but it was a malfunction; Capt. Arthur Shepard and his men were all present and accounted for. Mike called for more ambulances, made sure enough emergency medical technicians were standing by for men who'd surely be wracked by carbon monoxide. Fire Alarm told him six ambulances were waiting.

George Zinkus, Mike's aide, was monitoring the battle against the fire, keeping Mike briefed on the battle fatigue. At 7:02, he told Mike they needed more men. "We could use a fresh crew over here," he said from the C-side stairs. "Engine 7 just came down. We are at the other stairway."

"Okay," Mike said. "We got 'em here."

"Have them follow that two-and-a-half on the first floor all the way around to us."

Then Fenton was calling him again. "Command to Interior, Chief McNamee."

"Go ahead, Command."

"Do you need any additional lines in there?"

A brief pause. "Say that again?"

"Do you need any additional lines in there?"

"Negative. We have enough lines. The focus right now is on the search."

"Ten-four. I got men out here now. Do you want any additional help or need relief up—"

Mike cut him off. "Fresh crews with masks. We're going to rotate people in."

"Repeat that message."

Too late. Tommy Spencer was calling Mike on the radio. "Stand by, Command," Mike told Fenton. "Ladder 2, repeat your message."

"Chief," Tom said, "are all the people accounted for, out of the building? Ladder 2 and Engine 3 are on the fifth floor, still searching."

"Okay."

"Are they accounted for?"

The words were lost in the cacophony of the fire, drowned out by flames and saws and hoses and static. And Mike was distracted by other tasks. The men fighting the fire needed to be relieved. He steered a team from Engine 8 through the first floor, toward the C stairs, radioed George that relief was on the way.

Paul Brosnihan, on the other hand, was trying to locate his lieutenant. He'd been dispatched to rip the plywood out of the stairwell windows, open more holes so the smoke could cough out into the open air. Doug Armey, one of Sully's men, had peeled off to help. With that task done, he wanted to find Tom Spencer. He called him twice before he got an answer.

"Ladder 2, go ahead."

"Tommy, did you come up the stairway, four flights?"

"We came up the stairwell," Tom said. "We're on the fifth floor."

"What is your location on the fifth floor?"

"Good question."

"Repeat," Brosnihan said.

"We're doing a sweep."

"Are you near the front side of the building or the rear?"

"I believe that we are in the front part of the building."

"Okay," Brosnihan said. "I've got myself and Firefighter Armey."

It was 7:05. Paul Brotherton and Jerry Lucey had been lost for almost twenty minutes, buddy-breathing for fifteen. At the bottom of the stairs, Mike was entering a desperate phase. He was still calm, detached, his emotions stripped away from his technical duties. But he knew only a miracle—a fortuitous air pocket, an obscured window—would allow Paul and Jerry to still be breathing, still be alive. Yet it was difficult to monitor the search. The men who tromped down the stairs briefed him on the conditions above—bad and getting worse—but there were others, more than a dozen of them, scattered throughout the warehouse. The only way to keep track of all of them, to gather their field reports, was over the radio. And he couldn't hear the damned thing. Saws screeched through wood and metal, hoses gushed, fire hissed like a herd of dragons.

"Stop with saw," he snapped into the radio. "We can't hear the radio transmissions. Stop with that saw."

Sully was finally coming down the stairs, emerging from the fog like a dirty wraith. He told Mike how hot it was, how dark, how he couldn't hear any PASS alarms, couldn't stay any longer in the heat and the smoke. Then Fenton was back on the radio.

"Go ahead," Mike said.

"Do you need relief for Engine 3 and Ladder 2?"

"Engine 3 is already exiting." He was looking at Sully, knew it was true.

Tom Spencer and Tim Jackson were still five floors up. At eight minutes past seven, Spencer pressed his talk button. "Ladder 2 to Command."

Fenton answered, "Command. Go ahead, Ladder 2."

"Chief, get a company up the stairwell to the fifth floor," Tom said. "We can't locate the stairwell. Or give us some sign as to which way to go. We are running low on air and want to get out of—"

The transmission was cut off. For three and a half minutes, an agonizingly long time in three-hundred-degree darkness with a preciously limited supply of oxygen, the airwaves were cluttered, either with open microphones—guys hitting their buttons by mistake or at the same time as someone else—or chatter about where to put another hose. Tom Spencer finally held his button, raised his voice, demanded attention. "Ladder 2 to Command!"

"Command," Fenton said. "Go ahead."

"Send somebody up the stairwell to the fifth floor. Stand in the doorway and start singing."

"Repeat that message."

Mike patched in. "Slow it down a little."

"Get somebody up in the stairwell to the fifth floor," Tom said again. He was calm, almost serene, as if he knew fear was an extraneous emotion, something that could only distract him, blur his concentration, sap his strength. "Have them stand in the opening and yell. We can't find the door to the stairs."

Fenton still couldn't hear it. "Repeat the message," he said. "We can't understand it. Repeat the message clearly."

Sully jumped in. Sully had good ears and a fresh bottle of air. "Engine 3 has the message, Chief. We're going to the fifth floor, to the stairway, to lead them."

It was 7:13. Sully stumbled up the stairs, feeling his way through the murk. When he'd counted five floors, he stopped, stood stone still, closed his eyes because he always listened better that way. He strained to catch the faintest sound, the shuffle of knees against concrete or the shriek of a PASS alarm or the static cackle of a radio.

No sound. So he yelled, stretched his lungs, forced bottled air over his vocal cords until he thought they might rupture. "This way! This way!" He banged on the railing with his ax, making noises he hoped would carry through the din of the fire. Then he closed his eyes again, listened some more. Nothing rose above the awful monotony of flames.

Tom Spencer and Tim Jackson were halfway across the building, closer to the firewall than the stairwell. The racket Sully made was swallowed in the distance between the two men, devoured by the din of the fire, absorbed by the smoldering insulation in the thick walls. Tom listened, though, strained to hear a ping or a yell. For three minutes he waited in the dark, soaked with sweat, dizzy from the heat and his own shallow breathing. He heard nothing but the roar of an inferno.

Fifty-six seconds after 7:15, Tom spoke into his radio. "Ladder 2 to Command," he said. "We're done—"

The transmission was cut off, another radio squelching it. But Tom's voice had still been calm, level, maybe resigned. And the words were so soft that no one even heard them above the chaos.

14

WHEN JOE MCGUIRK DESIGNED THE KITCHEN IN THE PINK house with the green shutters that he'd built for Linda, he put the sink in the corner, under a window that looked out over the deck that surrounded the pool in the backyard and the lawn where he jogged behind his lawnmower on summer mornings. The countertops radiated out from the sink, perpendicular to each other, the right side stretching ten feet until it butted up against the refrigerator. To the left, the counter was broken by the stove, then continued to the far wall. A small television was plugged into an outlet at the end, beneath a cabinet.

Linda turned on the TV a few minutes after seven o'clock, but only for background noise while she washed dishes in the sink. She was humming to herself, spiced with a dab of holiday cheer. After Joe had left for the station, she'd spent the late afternoon and early evening addressing Christmas cards, eighty-five of them. It was a splendid card, a photograph of Everett and Emily at Disney World, standing in front of oversize cartoon characters, Pluto, Goofy, Mickey, and Donald all cast in ice-white plastic. On her head, Emily had a pair of white mouse ears. They'd spent eight days there before Thanksgiving, ran through seven thousand dollars. Linda wasn't sure if they could afford it. Looking at the photo a few weeks later, she didn't care. "Wishing You Holiday Happiness," the card read. "Love, Joe, Linda, Everett, and Emily."

She took a break at about six to feed the kids, three of them because Everett's friend Dan was over. They were in the basement rumpus room, rumpusing. After she finished the dishes, Linda would put Emily to bed, address a few more cards, then ride herd on the boys, get them to settle down enough to go to sleep.

She wiped a sponge across a knife, cleaned specks of butter from the blade. Linda heard a voice over her shoulder, distant and tinny. A reporter on the television. The sentences sounded like fragments, phrases, her ears picking up scattered facts. *Four-alarm fire.* She wheeled toward the screen. *Worcester Cold Storage.* She saw a spectacular sight: a black square, the warehouse, dominated the screen. At the bottom, above the cab of a firetruck, a patch of tangerine light tumbled from the lower windows. More orange played across the top of the screen, but a different shade, muted, hidden by a mushroom of smoke. Embers, bright yellow that faded to white-hot ash, twirled in the sky.

Two firefighters missing.

Her hands went numb, then her arms. Her knees wobbled. Her chest seized, her insides calcified, brittle, waiting to shatter. Her heart beat once, twice. She felt it, the collapse, everything from her neck to her hips—her lungs, her stomach, her very soul—disintegrating, dropping, shards tearing and ripping.

Joe was dead. She knew it, believed it.

She thought of the brotherhood. Joe was always going on about the goddamned brotherhood. He was the youngest of ten, three girls and seven boys. "Like you don't have enough brothers already," she used to tease him. "You had to go out and get a thousand more." Joe would laugh. But he'd die for the brotherhood. He knew that. Linda knew that.

Her eyes stung, the picture blurry now through tears pooling in her eyes. Then Emily was at her side, reaching for her hand. "Mommy, what's wrong?"

Linda blinked, squeezed the tears back, wiped at her face. "Oh, there's just a big fire," she said. She looked at her little girl for a moment. Reflexively, she snapped off the television. "Why don't you go brush your teeth," she said. "C'mon, it's time to get ready for bed."

She followed Emily up the stairs and steered her toward the bathroom. Linda went into her and Joe's bedroom and turned on the television. The images were surreal, the stuff of nightmares and Hollywood. The wide shots revealed the immensity of the blaze: the interstate underlining the WORCESTER COLD STORAGE AND WAREHOUSE CO. sign, giving the building scale, which in turn put the fire and smoke blowing out the top in awesome perspective. The flames leaped at least thirty feet above the roof, then tumbled over on themselves, balls of fire rolling into the night. Yet the tight shots were worse, the zooms in through the few open windows, the ones on the second floor where the fire was contained. There were sheets of flame, all of them oddly horizontal, luminous orange waves outlined by a golden brown. She couldn't see what was actually burning, no dark shapes, nothing from which the fire appeared to take root. It was as if the flames were independent entities, erupting only from air, a thousand of them, writhing together, fighting for space and fuel.

She pulled her knees into her chest. Her eyes began to sting again. She blinked. A tear dripped down her cheek.

She heard Emily in the hallway, then in the bedroom next to her. "Mommy . . ."

"Oh, Em . . ." Another tear fell. Emily had Joe's eyes, his mouth. Oh, he'd spoil her one of these days. His pretty princess.

That was Emily's favorite game, Pretty, Pretty Princess. Joe would play it with her, put a tiara on his head, clip on earrings, wrench plastic rings onto his thick fingers and bright bangles onto his wrists, drape strings of big plastic beads around his neck and over his belly.

Linda swallowed hard, wiped her eyes. "There's a really bad fire, Em. A really, really bad fire."

Emily crawled onto the bed with her mother, snuggled into her arms. Linda tried not to weep, watching the television, praying for a sign.

A fireman cut through the live shot. She recognized the face, the heavy eyebrows, the Victorian mustache. Sully. Her whole body twitched, a spasm of joyous relief. "Look, look," she said, pointing at the screen.

"What?" There was worry in Emily's voice. Sully was gone from the shot.

"Oh, honey, it's not going to be Daddy. I saw his lieutenant. I just saw his lieutenant. And Daddy can't be in the building without his lieutenant. Daddy's going to be okay."

The stairwell was sweltering, almost painfully hot, the smoke bubbling at more than 300 degrees. John Sullivan stood his ground on the fifth-floor landing, fought against the scorching draft that raced up from below, black gases rushing up through the open bulkhead. He yelled for five minutes, banged on the railing, made as much noise as he could, a sonic beacon to guide the men trapped inside.

When he'd gone up after Tom Spencer and Tim Jackson, he'd misheard the transmission. He thought men from Ladder 4 were lost. At eighteen minutes after seven, he got on the radio. "Engine 3 to Ladder 4, Captain Dolan."

"Ladder 4 answering."

▲ Jerry Lucey used to tell his wife, Michelle, that his favorite movie, *Backdraft,* was badly flawed. "That's so fake," he'd say during the bright orange fire scenes. "If they really showed what it was like, the screen would be black." From left, John, Jeremiah III, and Michelle. *[Bruce Davidson/Magnum]*

▶ Firefighter Jerry Lucey (left) twisted an ankle or sustained some other minor injury only when his partner, Paul LaRochelle (right), was on vacation. Paul would tell him, "It's because I wasn't there." *[Chris Gould]*

▲ Searchers found the sterling silver medallion of St. Florian that Jay Lyons wore around his neck. His sister Kathy—flanked by his mother, Joan, and his father, James—wears it now. *[Bruce Davidson/Magnum]*

▶ "When I'm driving Engine 3," Jay Lyons told his father, "I'm living every boy's fantasy." Jay encouraged that fantasy among schoolchildren who would visit the station, giving them a guided tour and posing for pictures with each child. *[Peggy Pierce]*

▲ Lt. Tom Spencer worked three jobs but still found time to go on long hikes with his wife and teach his kids about baseball and the constellations. "I would never use my job as an excuse to not do something with the kids," he told Kathy. From left, Daniel, Casey, Kathy, and Patrick. *[Bruce Davidson/Magnum]*

◀ Tom Spencer was working his last night on Ladder 2. He expected to be transferred to a nine-to-five job in the fire-prevention unit so he could spend the weekends with his wife and three children.

▲ Joe McGuirk named his construction company
McGuirk & Son after his boy, Everett, was born in
1989. Joe played dress-up with his daughter,
Emily, and built a pink house with green
shutters for his wife, Linda.
[Bruce Davidson/Magnum]

▶ Firefighter Joe McGuirk spent seventeen
years trying to follow his father and big
brother onto the fire department. The
Worcester Cold Storage fire was the first big
one he'd been in.

▶ Firefighter Paul Brotherton had his first date with his wife, Denise, the same week in 1983 that he started his fire department training. Sixteen years later, he still kept the tickets from that date in his wallet.

▼ When Paul Brotherton died, his brother firefighters stepped in to help his widow and six sons cope. Joe LeBlanc, center, was Paul's mentor on and off the job, and Tom Dwyer, top right, was his partner, watching his back inside the flames. Paul's sister, Kim, right, whom Paul raised after their parents died, gave birth to a son she named for her brother a few weeks after the fire. Denise Brotherton, holding her nephew, is on the left. *[Bruce Davidson/Magnum]*

◀ Firefighter Tim Jackson, who did two tours in Vietnam before he joined the Worcester Fire Department in 1972, tended lilacs and hydrangeas in the yard of the house where he lived with his third wife, Mary.

▼ Tim shielded Mary from the dangers of firefighting. He discouraged her from even watching the movie *Backdraft*. "You don't need to see that," he'd tell her. *[David Conlin/courtesy of Mary Jackson]*

John Sullivan sniffed the air early on the night of December 3, 1999. "A big one coming," he promised Jay Lyons. "Three alarms. I can smell it." A few hours later, he was screaming through the smoke, desperately trying to lead lost men to safety. *[Bruce Davidson/Magnum]*

▲ District Chief Mike McNamee pointed at Worcester Cold Storage as he drove past it two weeks before the fire. "That building scares me," he told his wife, Joanne. "That building scares the shit out of me." *[Bruce Davidson/Magnum]*

▶ District Chief Randy Chavoor (right, with his brother-in-law, Lt. Jay Grokaitis) thought the night would end with him teasing Jerry Lucey about getting lost. He never suspected that one man, let alone six, would get lost inside Worcester Cold Storage. *[Chris Gould]*

▲ In the months after the fire, dozens of Worcester firemen memorialized their fallen brothers with tattoos. From left, Kevin Reando, Rich Roy, Gary Williams, Lt. Dave Halvorsen, who was in charge of Rescue 1 the night of the fire, Stephen "Yogi" Connole, who found the flames on the second floor, and Capt. Robert A. Johnson, who ran Engine 1, which was the first pumper on the scene. *[Bruce Davidson/Magnum]*

"Chief, I'm in the doorway." Wrong rank. Sully corrected himself. "I mean, Captain, I'm in the doorway on the fifth floor."

Ten seconds passed. Captain Dolan was trying to decipher the message. "Chief," he said, "who's in the doorway at the fifth floor? Command, they're calling Ladder 4. We're not . . . We're on the third floor."

"Are you still looking for the door?" Sully asked. He wasn't sure if he should stay on the fifth or drop to the third. "Captain, are you still looking for the doorway out?"

Jack Fenton cut in, called Sully. "Command to Engine 3, Lieutenant Sullivan."

"Chief, this is Engine 3. Ladder 4 was looking for someone in the doorway. Are they all set?"

Dolan got back on the air. "It was Ladder 2, not Ladder 4."

"Okay, ten-four, Cap." Damn. Did Ladder 2 get out? He hadn't heard any more broadcasts from Spencer, nothing to indicate he was either still in trouble or safely down. Sully knew he couldn't last much longer in those conditions. He was already running low on air. He had to retreat.

At 7:20, he started down the stairs. "Engine 3 is coming out," he said into his radio. He wanted to make sure the brass knew where he was, didn't send anyone in looking for him.

He came out the Arctic Street side of the building. The heat from his gear rose into the December air, condensed, surrounded him in steam that looked like smoke, only colder and whiter. He turned the corner onto Franklin, passed in front of one of the television cameras recording the scene, walked briskly toward his truck parked under the highway for a fresh air tank. The cold night felt good on his face.

The air tanks were on the back of Engine 3. He grabbed one, then counted how many were left. All of them, except the first five his men had strapped on before they went in the first time. Jay and Joe hadn't come out for a second one. Sully realized he'd lost track of them, that he hadn't seen either one since he told Jay to shut down the truck.

His throat seized. Sully had been so focused on finding Paul and Jerry and then leading Ladder 2—what he thought was Ladder 4—to safety that he'd let his own men get away from him. He trusted Jay, because Jay was a damn good fireman. Jay would take care of Joe. But he was their lieutenant. A lieutenant is always supposed to know where his men are.

Sully lurched around the truck, jogged back toward the warehouse. He fixated on one thought: he had to find Jay and Joe. He had to see them, know they were all right.

The fire was winning, advancing, claiming the warehouse floor by floor. The flames were still pinned down, men with great streams of water beating them back, containing the worst of the inferno to the center of the building. But nothing could stop the heat, even slow it down. The sixth floor had been impenetrable for almost thirty minutes, a broiling black oven. The coats and pants firemen wore were heat-resistant, but nothing could protect a man from 400 degrees of damp heat. His skin would begin to roast, and his lungs would wheeze, gasping hot oxygen, his throat clutching with each scorching breath. Even for men desensitized to extreme temperatures, inured to the pain, functioning in such an environment was physically impossible. The body simply refused to respond to signals from the brain, which would be distorted by dehydration and disorientation anyway.

The fourth and fifth floors had been lost soon after the sixth. Men fought their way up the stairs, the now-opened windows offering only the slightest relief, making the journey possible if still excruciating. But they couldn't push more than a few feet past the doorways.

Bob Mansfield was back at the bottom of the stairs, a fresh tank strapped to his back, waiting to be rotated back up. Mike McNamee pointed at him, Charlie Gallagher from Ladder 5, Tom Dwyer from Rescue 1, and another man whose soot-smeared face he didn't recognize. "Go to the third floor," Mike told them. He looked each man hard in the eye as he spoke, as if he were studying them, looking into their heads, making sure they understood. "Stay together and stay on the ropes. Get out before your low-air alarms go off."

Bob let the chief probe his eyes. He was scared, knew what he was going into. But Mike's stare, the cool resolve in his voice, took the edge off Bob's nerves. "If he can be calm," Bob told himself, "if he can get through this, so can I."

Tommy Dwyer led. He slipped past Mike and into the stairwell, three men behind him. They could see at first, climbing the first flight of stairs. At the second floor, their heads disappeared into the smoke, the cloud banking down, swallowing them step by step. Just beyond the landing, the man in front of Bob vanished completely. He knew he was there only because he could feel him on the rope.

They regrouped at the third floor, double-checked that all four of them were together. Tommy felt for the rope, found it tied to the railing. He held it up, let each man behind him grab on. That was their lifeline, the thin strand that would save their lives. "All right," he yelled. "Stay close. When I say go, we go."

They stepped through the doorway and dropped to their knees. Bob felt the heat slam into him, like the concussion from a large bomb only steady, a constant push instead of a single pulse. The four of them edged forward. Bob thought he was melting or exploding or both. For a minute or maybe five— time was a blur—they shuffled along the floor. The temperature seemed to rise each inch farther in.

"We can't get in there," Tommy yelled over his shoulder. "It's just too bad. Back it out, back it out."

The four men bailed out, retreated down the stairs. At the bottom, Tommy began to brief Mike, tell him how much more territory they'd lost. Ten more men were gathered around him, jaws clenched, eyes grim. They were stacked up at the door, waiting to go back up, almost demanding to be let in.

Bob knew no one was going to make it up the stairs. He grabbed Charlie's arm, jerked his head toward the loading dock. "Let's go to the roof," he said.

Charlie followed him to Ladder 5, which was parked on Arctic Street, its stick extended over the cab and up to the roof. They found a rope, climbed to the top, stepped on the roof. Black smoke blew out of the stairwell bulkhead. They ducked past it. Bob straightened the rope, tied it off to a post. He noticed Charlie staring at the parapet where the firewall poked up.

"Bob," he said, "look at that."

The roof was bubbling more violently now, the tar rising in boils, each bursting and settling back to the pitch. A bad sign. The heat below was intense, rising to the temperature at which metals are smelted. The roof was going to give out, melt away, let the flames burst through. They didn't have much time before they would have to get back to the ground.

"All right, Charlie," Bob said. "Hang on to the rope. This is just like in diving, okay? Tug it once to ask if I'm okay. One tug means I am. Two tugs means send more rope. Three tugs means I'm in deep shit, come and get me."

Charlie nodded that he understood. Bob fixed his mask to his face and walked into the smoke, felt for the stairs. The force of the fire was worse from this angle. The smoke came out like a hard wind, a hurricane of soot and ash and vaporized petroleum, and the sound was deafening. He thought of a locomotive, imagined an iron engine barreling up the stairs, no headlamp to tell him it was coming, taking dead aim to crush him.

Bob went slowly, feeling for the stairs, clinging to the rope with one hand, carrying a flathead ax in the other. He made it down one set of risers, turned ninety degrees to the next, then traversed the third to the landing. He felt his way around. The rope jerked in his hand. Not a tug, not Charlie checking on him. It was stuck, tangled somewhere behind him. Bob back-tracked, following the rope until he found the snag. He loosened it, pulled some more rope down from above. He'd lost time. How much, he wasn't sure.

It took him precious more seconds to descend to the fifth floor. When he found the door, he swung his ax against the railing, steel against steel, a deep clanging. He stopped swinging, listened. He heard Charlie hollering, "Bob, keep doing that. They can hear you. Keep doing that!"

Bob wound up again and swung, got into a rythym. *Bang. Bang. Bang.* His pores were screaming, dumping sweat. His chest ached. He swung until the muscles in his arms screamed. "God, let someone hear this," he whispered. "Let someone hear."

No one came. He descended to the fourth floor, pounded on the railing down there. He heard no more yelling. Bob was getting dizzy from the heat and the noise. He wondered how much air was left, decided not enough. Suddenly, he was scared, the same fear he'd had in that burning cellar. He had to get out, was sure he wouldn't if he didn't go now, right then. He grabbed the rope, pulled himself up the stairs, moving faster than he did on the way down, faster than he thought he could. When he got to the roof, he was still enveloped in smoke, blackness all around him. The ladder was gone, hidden behind the cloud. He ran to the right, toward the edge of the roof, spotted the ladder, started down, Charlie with him.

At the bottom, on the back of Ladder 5, Bob went numb. He

was exhausted and dehydrated, but he was also scared, certain he'd fled death, escaped a step ahead of it.

And then he was ashamed. *What if they'd heard me? What if they were almost there?* He put his head in his hands. *What if I left them to die?*

John Sullivan circled the warehouse, looking at faces stained with ash and sweat. Jay and Joe would have gone inside, that much he was certain of. And Jay would have gotten them both out. Jay was ballsy, maybe wanted too badly to be a hero, but he was smart, seasoned. He wouldn't risk losing Joe.

"Have you seen Jay or Joe?" Sully asked an engine man. Then a ladder man, another lieutenant, every fireman he saw. Each shook his head, and Sully asked the next one more frantically. He went around the building again. Jay would be there, somewhere. Maybe by the door. He knew how it would end, Jay lumbering out, Joe next to him, both of them all soot and steam, Jay grinning. "Man, that was fucked up, huh?"

No one had seen either man all night, not since Sully left them at the truck. It didn't make sense. Mike McNamee was at the bottom of the stairs almost constantly, and when he stepped out to get a better look at the building, other men were stationed there, waiting their turn to go up. Maybe Jay had managed to sneak past them. There was one other door, at the A-D corner, but no one was using it. If he'd forced it open, then he was on his own inside.

He clicked his radio at 7:27. "Engine 3 to Engine 300, Jay or Joe, call in."

No answer. He kept moving, stalking the fireground, hunting his men. Three minutes later, he tried again. "Engine 3 to Engine 300."

Nothing.

He saw McNamee on Arctic Street, checking the building again. Sully sprinted toward him. "Mike, I can't find Jay or Joe," he said, his voice shaking. "I've been around this building three times, and I can't find them. No one's seen them."

Mike stared at him, didn't say a word. His mind spun. Paul and Jerry had been missing for forty-five minutes. No one had heard from Tom Spencer and Tim Jackson for twenty. The temperature inside, in the belly of the building, had soared to 3,000 degrees, almost twice as hot as a crematorium. And none of those men had enough air to last more than a half hour.

Sully stared back. He was pale, even through the grime on his face, and his eyes were wet. *They're dead.* The phrase scratched across his mind, over and over. *They're dead. All those fucking guys, they're all fucking dead.* His legs turned to jelly. He wanted to vomit. He spun away from Mike, shuffled to his truck, robotic and numb. He watched the fire, the flames dancing in the office windows, the smoke and steam rising from the roof. It was too much to witness. He went to the back side, put the truck between himself and the warehouse, as if he was hiding from the building, wishing it away. Then he fell to his knees and began to pray. Sully wasn't a religious man, but he didn't know what else to do.

15

BARELY MORE THAN AN HOUR AFTER THE FIRST ALARM HAD sounded for an innocuous plume of smoke seeping from the roof of Worcester Cold Storage, sixty-three men were battling a hellfire inferno. Four alarms had aleady been struck, and more men were coming. Worcester firemen were called at home on their night off, the chief of the department, Dennis Budd, was paged away from dinner with his wife, and crews from sleepy bedroom towns like Paxton and Auburn were speeding into the city. A truck from Millbury was bringing a thermal imager, a camera that can see through smoke, the kind of high-tech gear Worcester couldn't afford.

Shortly after seven o'clock, District Chief Randy Chavoor was holed up at the South Division station. Normally, the second district chief in the city reports on the third alarm, which had been sounded at 6:40, but he had to wait for a man to relieve him at the firehouse. The southern district has always burned more readily and heavily than the rest of Worcester; leaving half the city, eighteen square miles, unsupervised was a dangerous proposition, no matter how ferociously a fire might be burning in the north.

Besides, Randy wasn't worried. After twenty-three years on the job, he had a pretty good idea how an empty warehouse would burn. He could write a script, crib the basic operation from the textbooks, add the details from experience. The ladder guys would enter and vent, the rescue men would sweep, the engine men would soak the flames. If it got away from them, if the red stuff overpowered the wet stuff, the firemen would simply regroup, fall back to a safe distance and open up the big guns. Surround and drown. Maybe some of the guys would have to rub salve onto their ears to soothe a minor burn, and the locker rooms would echo with wracking coughs, soot being hacked out of weary lungs. But everyone would shower and have coffee.

He'd monitored the fire all night, since he'd tried to swipe the alarm from Mike McNamee. After he'd left Grove Street, he had his aide, Franny Baldino, park on Grafton Street, a block or so from the building, so he could watch the attack. He saw seven shiny red trucks and two dozen men in heavy coats surrounding a big brick cube that was leaking a soft puff of gray smoke. He'd seen the same scene a hundred times before. He got bored and told Franny to take him back to South Division.

The radio chatter hadn't spooked him, either. When he'd heard Jerry call for help, say he was running out of air, Randy grinned. *Man,* he thought, *I am gonna bust his balls tonight.* He could write that script, too, because he knew Jerry, knew what kind of fireman he was, which was a good one.

He'd met him back in 1992, when Randy was the captain in charge of Rescue 1 and Jerry still had the green shield of a rookie bolted to his helmet. (The green made a recruit easy to spot on the fireground; there was no sense sending a man into a burning building before he'd gotten some experience under his belt.) Jerry had introduced himself, told Randy he wanted the open slot on the rescue truck. The veterans were amused. Guys waited years, sometimes decades, to get on rescue. And a green-shield thought he was waltzing in? Randy had to admit he'd never heard of such a thing. Then again, he'd never known a rookie with the stones to ask a captain for a job, either. He took him on. "I believe I can make someone a good firefighter," he told the other men when they complained. "But no one can make a good attitude. The kid's got a good attitude."

Randy gave him a hard time early on. Shortly after Jerry joined the truck, Randy leaned out a window on the second floor of a burning triple-decker, felt his helmet slip off his head, watched it disappear into the bushes below. He sent the green-shield to find it, made him root around in the shrubbery, miss all the action inside. "I can't fucking believe it," Jerry groused to anyone who'd listen. "My first big fire, and that fucker made me look for his fucking helmet."

Jerry learned the craft quickly and well. Within a couple years, he was moonlighting at the Massachusetts Firefighting Academy, support work mostly, but passing on some of what he'd picked up on the job. The past few years, he'd been partnered with Paul LaRochelle, another good man. Sick and Twisted, they called themselves. "I'm Sick," Paul would say. "And he's Twisted." It was a good schtick. Rescue partners were tight like that, like brothers. Each entrusted his life to the other, believed he would survive because his partner wouldn't let him die. Like that night Paul was foundering in a kitchen, smoke falling across his face mask, the linoleum melting beneath his knees. "I can't find the door," he screamed, and Jerry answered, soothing, steady. "I got it, Paul, I got it. Come this way."

Jerry and Paul LaRochelle got out that night because rescue men always got out. Randy had never lost a man when he ran the truck, had never heard of any truck losing any man in all his years with the department. So Randy knew Jerry would get out of Worcester Cold Storage. And when he saw him later, after the warehouse had been reduced to smoldering rubble and steamy puddles, he would swat his shoulder and make a face at him. "What's the matter with you, Jerry?" he'd tease. "Didn't I teach you better than that? *Real* rescue guys don't get lost, you know." Then they would both laugh, even if the sting from the smoke made their throats hurt.

Chief Budd had struck a fifth alarm at 7:26. Ninety seconds later, Randy got out of Car 4, his Ford Expedition, and started to cross Franklin Street. He saw Mike McNamee ahead of him, just off the curb, a sillhouette in his off-white officer's coat. He reached out a hand as he passed, never broke stride as he patted Mike on the shoulder. "Hey, Mike, you got those two guys out, right?"

He took two more steps before Mike answered.

"Randy. No."

Randy stopped short, jerked, snapped at the waist, as if a ghost had swung a two-by-four into his gut. He twisted around, but slowly, the air around him suddenly sticky and thick, like molasses. His stomach hurt.

"What?"

"Randy . . ." Mike blinked hard, swallowed. "Randy," he said again, his voice a hoarse whisper, "it's not two. It's six."

The two district chiefs stared at each other. Randy tried to catch his breath, force air through his throat, form words with his numb tongue and lips. His shoulders slumped and his hands tingled and his head buzzed, his brain trying to reconcile what he'd heard with what he knew to be true, which was: firemen were immortal. That was dogma, the underlying tenet of their collective faith. Men went into burning buildings, stood firm against a force of nature—against the fundamental element of the entire universe—only because they knew they would not die. Sure, they talked about the danger. They recited romantic drivel about how every alarm could be their last and they shellacked "The Fireman's Prayer" to pieces of oak they hung in their half baths off their kitchens and they told women in bars that they wanted to die with their boots on like real American cowboys and they chiseled the name of every old retiree who finally dropped dead at eighty-seven into granite monuments surrounded by petunias and geraniums. But none of that was real. None of them believed it, not in his soul. No man would go to work if he expected to die before sunrise.

Randy wheeled, his legs moving automatically. One step, a second, then faster, running toward the building. Six men were still inside, needed to be saved. If he let them die, then a part of him, a piece of every man there, would die, too.

Mike watched Randy head for the building. He felt a shudder go through him, squirmed under his coat. He had to focus, concentrate on tactics. Paul and Jerry were probably dead, but the other four still had a chance. Tom Spencer and Tim Jackson were two of the best, almost fifty years of experience between them, and most of Tim's had been on Rescue 1. Jay and Joe weren't as seasoned, but they were good firemen, strong young guys. If anyone could survive inside that building, Mike would put his money on those four. It was his job to get them out, and not lose any more men doing it.

He hurried back into the building, to the bottom of the stairwell where a dozen men were staging, waiting to be sent back up. "Everybody stay here," he hollered at them, then kept running, forty feet across the first floor and out the rear loading door, to the platform on the C side of the warehouse. The fire was being fought mostly from that side, hoses slithering up the stairs to the second floor. The flames were advancing, but his men were keeping them essentially in check.

The radio system was breaking down, alarms sounding from random units. The microphones that men wore near their collars had emergency buttons on the side, but they weren't watertight. When they got wet, they shorted out, broadcast a priority emergency that stole a channel. Communication, already difficult, was becoming impossible. Mike could hear Fire Alarm telling Engine 1 to disable one of its radios, clear the air.

He sprinted back to the B stairs. The men were all waiting. Chief Budd was on the radio, calling him. "Go ahead," Mike said.

"Yeah, Mike, I've got a thermal imager down here from Millbury and I want to send it in. I'm bringing down an aerial scope on this side of the building, on the east side of the building, and we want a couple of guys down here to go in with them."

"Okay," Mike said. "Nobody in without lifelines, though. We want lifelines on everybody. We have ropes tied off upstairs."

The ropes were the only chance he had left. He realized the fire was winning, spreading superheated gases into the freezer rooms and corridors. If anyone let go of the lifeline, another man would be lost in murk. And if Tom, Tim, Jay, and Joe were alive, there was a slim possibility they would stumble across the lines, find their own way out.

"Ladder 2 to Ladder 2." He recognized Paul Brosnihan's voice. Eighty seconds ticked off. He heard it again. "Ladder 2 truck to Ladder 2."

Then Brosnihan was calling him. "Ladder 2's truck to Chief McNamee." Again. "Ladder 2's truck to Chief McNamee." He kept pressing the button. "Ladder 2 to Chief McNamee." Anxiety laced the words. "Ladder 2's truck to Ladder 2."

Brosnihan was desperately trying to get a response from his lieutenant. Mike joined in. "Command to Ladder 2, Lieutenant Spencer."

No answer. Mike Coakley tried, screamed into his microphone. "Ladder 1 to Ladder 2! Ladder 2!"

For a minute, Mike McNamee and Mike Coakley alternated broadcasts, each one more urgent, each one answered by silence.

Brosnihan got on the air at 7:40, pleading, his voice cracking. "Ladder 2 to any company on the fifth floor, to any company on the fifth floor." No one replied.

Mike couldn't continue on the radio. There were too many other men for whom he was responsible, scattered throughout the building, some holding the fire at bay, others making last-ditch efforts to explore the upper floors. Randy Chavoor was on the third floor with two other men, wanting to know where the Millbury guys were with the thermal imager. A man on the second floor reported that the flames had broken through the fire wall, had clawed across the second floor toward the B stairs. A rescue team called in, told Mike the stairs were impenetrable past the fourth floor. "Okay," Mike told them, "don't risk it. Back down."

Mike realized the building was claiming territory and more men, taking them two by two. If the fifth floor was gone, Tom Spencer and Tim Jackson were likely dead. Brosnihan knew it as well. Mike heard him on the radio again, a shriek this time, a choking, sobbing scream. "Ladder 2 to Ladder 2! Lieutenant Spencer!"

Mike counted ten seconds. Silence. He pushed his own button. "Interior to Ladder 2," he said. "Lieutenant Spencer, answer. Please."

He waited eight seconds, then tried Jay Lyons. "Interior to Engine 300. Interior to Engine 300."

The fire roared in his ears, the only sound he heard.

Minutes contracted into seconds, Mike's sense of time blurred by the chaos around him and the adrenaline surging through his veins. He was struck by the fact that he wasn't afraid. He was controlled, determined, processing information like a machine. But he was in uncharted territory, trying to make decisions in a situation he'd never experienced, never expected to face. The warehouse was going to be destroyed, that much was certain. On any other night, he would have withdrawn an hour earlier, let the flames feast on rotting timbers and fetid rubbish, devour the whole thing. Yet on no other night, not once in his twenty-seven years as a Worcester fireman, had six men gone missing. And never had any man been abandoned. *We always win,* he told himself. *The building might burn to ash, but everyone goes home. We win.*

There would be a point at which the danger of continuing the search would outweigh the promise of finding anyone, dead or alive. But when? Firemen had survived worse fires, dragged people out of more ferocious blazes, gone into infernos when the stakes weren't nearly as high. Paul Brotherton had once risked his life to save someone's pet parrot. A parrot! Mike knew none of his men would admit defeat, surrender and walk away. He couldn't, either, not if there was the faintest ray of hope.

Worcester Cold Storage was deteriorating more rapidly now. Engine 9 called in, announced the exterior walls appeared to be cracking, that the side closest to the highway looked like it might collapse. Mike absorbed all of the facts coming over the radio and from the men returning from above. But he had to see for himself, gauge with his own eyes and ears and skin how treacherous the situation had become. He bolted into the stairwell, felt for the railing, climbed the stairs. By the second floor, the heat was withering, wrapping around him, pressing on him like a vise. He kept moving. He cleared one riser to the third floor, turned, made it to the next step.

Then something blew up. He heard it first, felt it an instant later. The sound was the same as when a match touches the pilot light of a stove, only loud as thunder, a spasm of air expanding so fast and hard against the warehouse walls that the whole building shuddered. The railing vibrated beneath his gloved hand. He gripped it tighter, waiting for the explosion to subside.

Robert A.'s voice barked over his radio. "Can you confirm that someone just said part of this building collapsed?"

He was close, just above Mike in the stairwell. "Robert A.," he yelled. "I don't think so. But I think a large area just lit off." A flashover maybe, somewhere on the upper floors, all those molecules of melting petroleum finally reaching their ignition temperature, turning to fire.

Mike barreled down the stairs. None of the men at the bottom had balked, fled outside. They eyed him like expectant fathers, waiting to be given the order—the permission—to ascend again into the inferno. Mike paused, skimmed their faces. "Wait," he said. "Nobody goes up."

He ran across the floor again, toward the back door, out onto the loading dock. The night sky glowed above him, illuminated by flames shooting thirty feet into the air. He told men to start pulling hoses down the stairs, get them out of the building. In the background, he could hear Mike Coakley warning of another breach in the walls, a six-foot crack above Ladder 4. Chief Budd ordered the truck moved away. Randy Chavoor came on the radio. The men from Millbury had made it to the third floor, but the thermal imager malfunctioned, the extreme heat blanking out the screen, showing only a field of white-hot smoke.

"Command to Chief McNamee." It was Dennis Budd. "Mike, how you doing in there?"

"We're backing out the back," Mike said. "We got a report that the walls were weakening in the front. We are trying to back the lines out so we can use them. It's through the roof in the back, and it's going like hell right up the side. I think we're almost ready to go to an exterior attack."

Then he ran back to the B stairs, into the doorway, onto the first step, then back down to the pavement. The lieutenant from Engine 2, Jimmy Pijus, emerged at the bottom of the stairs, exhausted. "We couldn't make the third, Chief," he told Mike. "It's just too hot. We can't get past it."

Mike nodded. He trusted Jimmy, knew he'd push through any fire that didn't physically hold him back. He looked at the men arrayed in front of him. The faces were all familiar. The beads of sweat cutting streaks through the soot, the eyes stung red from the smoke, the jaws firmly clenched—he'd seen them all before. They'd been at 728 Main Street, when Walter Rydzewski snapped at him, ordered him to leave that mangled woman on the pavement, save the people who could still be saved. They'd been in that warehouse on Jacques Street, sitting in the hallway, gasping, amazed their lieutenant had gotten out alive. They'd been inside flaming triple-deckers and outside crumpled Buicks and next to wheezing old men clutching their ailing hearts. They'd sat with him in the mornings, clean-shaven and showered, drinking coffee, and in the evenings, carving roast beef and wiping gravy from their mustaches. They had wives and girlfriends and children and parents. They were his men, and he was responsible for all of them.

"No more," he said.

For one stunned moment, no one said a word. The white noise of the fire droned above, punctuated by snaps and pops and hisses. Then, as if a trigger had been pulled, the men surged forward in unison, stormed the stairwell. "They're still in there," someone yelled. "Goddamnit, they're still fucking in there!" The other men joined in, all of them yelling, pressing forward.

Mike spread his arms and legs, pressed his palms and his

boots against the jambs of the door, used his body as an X to block the path. "Listen to me!" he bellowed. "You listen to me!"

A break in the shouting, the men easing back, startled by Mike's tone. He swept their faces again. He saw hurt in their eyes, betrayal.

"You listen to me," he said again, more softly this time. "We've already lost six. We're not going to lose any more."

It was as if he'd thrown a great, crushing weight upon them. The men slumped before him, physically sagged, the same reflex of defeat he'd watched Randy go through thirty minutes earlier. But it was worse this time. Mike had said it out loud, made it true: *We lost six.* In his time, Worcester had never lost one.

"I want everybody out," he said. He got on the radio. "Command to all companies," he said. "Evacuate the building. Sound the evacuation signal. Evacuate the building."

A tremendous racket rose up from the streets, three blasts sounding from the horns on each of the trucks, the signal to abandon the building. Men filed out, walking slowly, hobbled by despair. It was over. The battle would continue for hours, but there wasn't anything left to fight for. Paul, Jerry, Tom, Tim, Jay, and Joe weren't coming out. All that was left to do was reposition the engines, circle the warehouse, pour water into the flames, wait for the fire to finally exhaust itself.

Dennis Budd found Mike on the street, standing with Randy Chavoor and a few other men. "Mike, get four guys together," he said. "I want to make one last push."

Mike started to answer. Randy cut him off. "You've been in there long enough," he told Mike. "I'll go."

Randy and three other men marched toward the loading dock, through the doors, up the stairs. They were going to the third floor, as high as they could hope to get. Maybe Tom and

Tim had been wrong. Maybe they'd been on three. Maybe they found their way down there.

They found the rope tied off on the landing. Four men dropped to their knees, began to crawl. They inched in, the heat slowing them down. Randy could hear the fire, hissing and snarling and spitting, the sound seeming to come from all around him, but he couldn't see anything except black, couldn't feel anything except a sheet of steam wrapped around his face, swirling around him like a heavy cloth. He shivered despite the temperature, a premonition washing over him. Thirty feet from the door, he called off the mission. "Let's go!" he yelled. "We don't belong in here."

No one argued. Each man pivoted, began scuttling toward the door. It was longer on the way out. Randy felt another shiver. *It's not done,* he thought. *The building's not done with us.* The smoke closed in on him, formed itself into a massive black paw, swept over his shoulders, grabbed him by the neck. He could feel it pulling, dragging him into its misty gullet, strangling him. *That's it. You're gonna die.* He struggled against it, crawled what felt like thirty feet. No door. Another twenty feet. Nothing. He wondered if the warehouse had chewed off the lifeline, tossed it into a corner, lured him into a trap.

He felt the ledge, the step up to the doorway. His mind had gotten to him, a trick, an illusion that made ten yards feel like one hundred. Drenched with sweat, shaking with relief, he barreled down the stairs with the other men. He saw Brosnihan at the bottom, tears streaking the big man's face, dripping around his mustache. He rushed toward Randy, toward the stairs, toward his lost lieutenant. Randy caught him, held him in a bear hug, felt him heaving with sobs.

"We gotta go," he said. "C'mon, we gotta get out of here."

Randy kept his arm around Bros, steered him out to the

street. They were the last men to leave Worcester Cold Storage. No one would be saved tonight.

Robin Huard felt a squeeze on his arm, turned, saw Mike Mc-Namee.

"Robin, will you go in with me?"

Robin was exhausted, felt he'd cheated death once tonight, knew Worcester Cold Storage was too far gone. But he liked Mike, respected him, believed he was the best incident commander in the city. He wouldn't let him go alone.

"Mike, if you're going, I'll go with you," he said. "But . . ." He paused, gathered the words. "But you know they're all dead."

"I know," Mike said slowly. "But we've got to try something. I've got to try one more time."

Robin understood. An officer never leaves his men. Not a marine on Hamburger Hill, not a fireman on the edge of hell. He would follow Mike in if he had to.

Dennis Budd intercepted them. "No more, Mike," he said. "No one else goes in."

Robin was relieved.

16

ARLIER THAT EVENING, JUST AFTER SHE'D EATEN HER DINNER, Joanne McNamee remembered she'd left a package in the back of the aging Volvo station wagon parked in front of the house. She went out the door off the dining room, through the garage, and out onto the driveway. The night seemed peculiar, a month out of season. The air was chilly but not uncomfortably cold, and the breeze that blew up from the south was mild, nothing like the biting winds that typically rustled the bare branches in early December.

She had noticed a familiar sound, a faint and plaintive wail, as she turned to go back into the house. She stopped to listen. Twenty-five years had passed since she sat in an apartment at the top of a hill, hearing the sirens from the streets below, whispering to her absent husband that he'd better not die, not now, not yet. They'd moved miles away, to a leafy neighborhood west of downtown, but the wind could still sometimes catch the echo, carry the howl into her living room or at least to her driveway. She didn't whisper to Mike anymore. She'd long ago accepted that her husband had chosen a dangerous trade, and with that knowledge came a certain anxiety, low-grade but constant. Eventually, she'd become immune to it.

The noise grew louder, the volume seeming to double. She couldn't tell how many trucks were involved, but by the chorus, the overlapping yowls and whoops, she guessed a second alarm had already been struck. A dozen trucks, all rolling at once. They could be headed for Main South, but they sounded closer. Northern district, she suspected. "Must be a big one," she thought.

She had listened only for a moment or two before going back into the house, where she picked up the phone in the kitchen and dialed the number for Central Station. She didn't bother calling Mike's private line in his cinder-block office because she assumed he'd be out. She called the watch room instead.

The fireman who answered confirmed that Mike was working a fire.

"What's burning?" she asked.

"Worcester Cold Storage."

She'd gripped the receiver more tightly, whitening her knuckles. She remembered driving past the warehouse only two weeks before, when Mike had pointed at it and told her how badly it scared him. She could hear him saying it again: *God, I hope we never catch anything in there.*

"Shit," she said into the phone. "All right. Well, tell him to call me when he gets in."

She hung up, leaned against the cream-colored tiles Mike had cemented to the countertop, let out a heavy sigh. Mike had been through worse nights. She remembered when he came home that morning in 1973, black, wet, and exhausted, stinking of ash and fire and haunted by ten dead civilians. She'd wanted to stay with him, hold him, tell him how she was frightened and relieved and grateful all at once, give in to all the emotions that could torture a fireman's wife. Mike had fallen asleep and she'd gone to work and she'd put it out of her mind. He came home, and that's all that mattered. Her mother's advice came back to her: *You don't borrow worry.* Tonight was no time to start.

There were dishes in the sink. Joanne decided they needed to be washed, right then, immediately. She turned on the kitchen faucet, rinsed the plates, stacked them in the dishwasher, wiped the good knives with a soapy sponge and set them on a rack to dry. Then she sat on the couch in the family room and turned on the television, which was next to the window. Through the lace curtains, she could see the lamplight across the street in the window of the house where Jay Lyons had grown up, where his parents still lived.

She knew Jay was working tonight. It was fascinating to think of him as a fireman, as a man, to realize how many years had gone by. In one frame of her memory, Jay was a lanky schoolboy delivering her newspaper. In the next he was a rowdy teenager drinking with his buddies in the parking lot of the synagogue behind her house; she could hear the empty beer cans tinkling on the blacktop through the screen of evergreens that separated her yard from the lot. Then he was a handsome high school senior who she trusted to baby-sit her daughters, who brought them stuffed animals on their birthdays. "If one of my girls ever brings home a boy half as nice as Jay," she'd told Mike once, "I'll be a happy woman."

At eight o'clock, she switched to NBC. She'd gotten hooked on *Providence*. As the opening credits rolled, a bold line of type scrawled across the top of the screen. A few words and phrases leaped out at her, seemed to be backlit, radiant. *Five-alarm blaze.* Her stomach knotted. *Worcester Cold Storage Warehouse.* Her mouth went dry. *Two firefighters missing.*

She dropped the remote, grabbed her keys off the counter, ran out the front door, not bothering to close it behind her. She jammed the key into the Volvo's ignition, dropped it into reverse, stomped the gas, hit the pavement, then sped up Saxon Road. *Mike's one of them,* she thought. *Mike would be in the building. Mike would be the first one in the building and the last one in the building. Mike's missing.* Then, the worst thought, one she'd never allowed herself to imagine: *Mike might be dead.*

The green foil crinkled when she wrapped it around the plastic pots, puckered into tiny metallic ridges that Kathy Spencer smoothed with her hands. She pressed firmly but gently, carefully avoiding the red leaves of the poinsettias that draped over the edge of the pots. She pressed gold foil around the next one, then red on the third, alternating iridescent holiday colors. It wasn't glamorous work, but it was relaxing. Kathy looked forward to every shift at the nursery, especially after Thanksgiving. She was good with plants, and the amaryllis bulbs and evergreen wreaths and holly garlands stirred her Christmas spirit, made the holiday seem literally alive.

She worked until eight o'clock, then drove home to pack for the trip to New York City in the morning. A pang in her stomach reminded her she hadn't eaten anything since the turkey sandwich Tom made for lunch. She stopped at a sandwich shop, ordered an eggplant parmesan grinder to go, then drove the rest of the way home. She gave the horn a short toot as she passed the house two doors from her own where Tom's parents lived, which was next to the one where his brother Mike lived. He was a Worcester fireman, too. Tom liked living close to his family, the whole clan clustered together. His father had bought a small fishing boat a few months earlier, and when the weather warmed up three generations of Spencer men—father and sons and grandsons—would drift across a pond hunting blue gill and bass.

It was almost eight-thirty when she put her sandwich down

on the kitchen counter. She picked up the phone and dialed the number for the Grove Street station. It was a habit, checking in with Tom at the station when she came home. And she had to call tonight, his last night running Ladder 2.

A staccato buzz vibrated the earpiece. Busy. She hung up, unwrapped her dinner. The phone rang.

"Hello?"

"Kathy?" One of her friends.

"Yeah."

"Did you know there's a big fire downtown?"

"Um . . . no." Kathy hadn't watched television, which had been broadcasting live shots from Worcester Cold Storage for more than an hour.

"Well," her friend said, "it's a really bad one."

"Okay." An awkward pause. "Thanks for calling."

Kathy had gotten calls like that before, and she'd never been rattled by any of them. She didn't worry about Tom or any other man on the job because experience had taught her that firemen always came home in the morning. Her father had been a Worcester fireman, and her uncle, too, and they always came home. The hardest part for her father had been giving up the job. The city forced him to retire the day he turned sixty-five, which was December 26, 1984. He could have taken off Christmas Day, but he wanted to work one more shift.

He was a big part of the reason Tom became a fireman. By his second year at UMass–Lowell, Tom knew he didn't want to continue with college. Kathy's father told him about fighting fires, a good job with good benefits and decent pay, enough to support his daughter and his grandchildren. Tom took the test, scored well, dropped out of school and joined the department in 1978. He'd gotten banged up in the past twenty-one years, but nothing serious except for the night he got lazy and, instead of moving a ladder over a couple of feet, he leaned way out to the side, slipped, and tore up his knee. Fact is, he'd done more damage playing baseball, fast-pitch hard-ball in an over-thirty league. "None of that sissy softball," he'd tell Kathy. Two knee operations and a broken thumb later, she finally convinced him that his baseball injuries were keeping him off the firetrucks.

Kathy scouted for her kids. Patrick, the oldest, was watching a video with his girlfriend in the basement rec room, where Tom kept his baseball encyclopedias and his Civil War books and, on a bench in the back, the wooden model of a schooner he was building, thin strips of veneer for the decking already soaked and pliable. Daniel, the youngest, was at a party. Kathy made a phone call, made sure he had a ride home. Casey, their daughter, joined her in the kitchen, where they talked about their trip in the morning while Kathy ate. Kathy's friend Cheryl, who was going with them, called to finalize their plans.

She looked at her watch. Ten o'clock. The early news was on, with a weather preview near the top of the hour. Kathy switched on the television in the living room.

The first bright image startled her. The screen was a swirl of black and orange, broken by the red-and-white flashes of the lights from the fire trucks. Flames twisted from the roof of a dark, hulking square. She would have known it was Worcester Cold Storage, would have recognized the shape and the highway running next to it, even if the logo painted near the roof had been burned away.

Her eyes widened. "Wow, that is a big one," she muttered.

She felt Casey next to her. "What is it, Mom?" There was worry in her voice.

"Just a big fire," Kathy said. "But look"—she pointed at the bottom of the screen, where Ladder 2 was clearly visible—"there's Daddy's truck. We're all set."

She glanced at her daughter, whose brow was creased. Kathy snapped off the televsion. "C'mon," she said brightly. "Let's go pack."

After the pizza dinner, Denise Brotherton ferried her oldest son to his basketball game and brought her next oldest so he could watch. Denise usually found a seat in the bleachers, too, but she couldn't stay tonight. She had to go home and cook platters of food for Kim's baby shower on Sunday.

Kim was technically her sister-in-law, but they were much closer than that would imply. That was curious, too, considering that Denise had been her surrogate mother, helping Paul raise her after Paul's parents had died. When she was younger, Kim's friends used to tell her how lucky she was, growing up with her brother in charge. They didn't know the half of it. Paul and Denise were still young enough to know about the kegs of beer kids lugged into the woods at Burncoat Park, young enough to remember what went on all night after the senior prom. Which is why Kim had to be home at eleven o'clock every night, even during her senior year in high school, and why Paul grounded her for five weeks when she stumbled in past dawn after prom.

She had lived with them until 1998, when she married her husband, Chris. Paul walked her down the aisle. A year later, he was the second person, after her husband, who Kim told she was pregnant. It was hard to tell who was more excited. "I'm going to redo a crib for the kid," Paul told her, which he did. Eight months later, he still had to stick fresh wallpaper on the nursery walls, but he'd already decided he would call the boy Nat, short for Nathan Paul. Kim drew the line at letting Paul coach her through labor. "There is no friggin' way you're coming into the delivery room with me," she said.

Denise got home at eight-twenty and went straight to the

kitchen to start cooking. The phone rang. It was one of Paul's cousins calling. "There's a big fire downtown," he said.

"Really? Where?"

"The cold storage building."

Denise thought for a second, scanned her memory of downtown, found Worcester Cold Storage. "Ugh," she said. "That's not good."

"Yeah, I know. I heard there were two men down."

"Oh, God. That's terrible." She gathered some bowls. "Look, I gotta go. I'll talk to you later."

It didn't occur to her that Paul would be missing. He was too careful, a stickler for safety. "You have to respect fire," he'd lecture his sons. "It'll destroy you in nothing flat it you don't respect it." When the medical runs increased, and with them the number of bleeders and pukers firemen had to deal with, Paul got himself innoculated against hepatitis B. She remembered him explaining why he was against doubling the size of their air tanks to a sixty-minute capacity. "No one should be inside a burning building for an hour," he'd told her. "That's way too long. You've got to get out of the heat, get rehydrated, rest." She knew Paul wouldn't be inside long enough to get lost, that he'd find his way out, bring his partner with him.

She hesitated, thought twice. Maybe she should call the station, just check in. She dialed the watchroom at Central Station. "It's Denise Brotherton," she said. "Is Paul in?"

"Nope." The voice was deadpan. "He's out on a run."

"Okay, just tell him I called."

She pressed the switch hook once, then dialed the number for the police department. "Hi, my name's Denise Brotherton—"

The line went dead. She found that odd, but assumed she'd been accidently disconnected. With a fire raging downtown, the police switchboard must have been overloaded with calls.

She put the phone back on the hook. It rang a moment

later, Paul's cousin calling again. "Denise, they're saying there's four guys missing."

A twitch in her stomach. Paul was careful, but he was also on the frontlines. He would have been one of the first men in. And if he'd gone in looking for someone else, maybe he wouldn't have been as careful, would have taken an extra chance, pushed harder.

"Denise, do you want to go down to the scene?"

"No," she said immediately. "Paul always told me if anything happened to him, the fire department would come to me. And no news is good news."

The broom whisked across the linoleum, sweeping soft clumps of freshly snipped hair into a neat pile. The phone in the salon rang. Michelle Lucey leaned the broom against the chair where she'd been cutting her clients' hair, reached for the receiver. It was Ralph, her brother.

"Michelle, there's a really big fire downtown," he said.

"Really?" She looked a the clock. A few minutes before nine. "Okay."

"Is Jerry working?"

"Yeah, he swapped on."

"It's a really big one."

"Okay," she said. "I believe you."

The conversation was short and inconsequential. Ralph often called when a particularly spectacular blaze ignited somewhere in the city, wanting to know if Jerry was working, if he was all right. He always was. In fact, Michelle worried more about his damned motorcycle than she did about him being a fireman. It was a retired police bike, a big white machine, and he rode it all year, even in the winter, pulling into the station with his cheeks red and raw from the wind. "You just have to have a Harley," she'd grouse at him. "More danger. What is it with you?"

"You know," Jerry would say, a touch of swagger in his voice, "my job is a lot more dangerous than a Harley."

And maybe that was true. He'd lost eight weeks one summer when he twisted his ankle on a step, and he complained about the soles of his feet hurting ever since he fell through a collapsing floor. Funny thing was, Jerry's partner, Paul LaRochelle, was always off when Jerry got hurt. "It's because I wasn't with you," Paul told him every time. "I'm telling you, you need me to watch your back."

Michelle picked up the broom and continued sweeping. She'd been cutting hair for twenty years. She made a good living at it, too, enough to practically support Jerry and the boys during the months when Jerry was laid off from the fire department. That's why they had a tiny house. Jerry wanted something they could afford on only one income, just in case one of them was out of work. They were doing all right now, though. Maybe next summer they'd blow out the side wall, build a family room over the garage and enlarge the basement. Jerry had already sketched out the plans.

She finished cleaning the salon, then picked up the phone again. She and Jerry were organizing the Christmas party for Group III, his regular shift, and she still needed a head count for the caterers. Mark Wyco hadn't confirmed yet. He was assigned to Group II, but had been close with Jerry ever since drill school. He was always invited. She called him at the Park Avenue station.

His voice was strained when he answered. "Michelle," he said, "where are you?"

"I'm at work. I'm just leaving now."

"Michelle, there's a really big fire," he said. A hitch, like he was swallowing. "Michelle, we might've lost six guys."

Her veins turned to ice. She struggled to form a word, force it past the lump in her throat. "Mark, Jerry's working tonight."

She let that hang there for a moment, gathered the oxygen for the next line. "Was he one of them?"

Mark was silent a beat too long. "I don't know," he said. "Michelle, go home. Now. Go home and make some calls."

The ice in her veins melted, began to boil, made her arms and her legs and her face tingle. Tears, salty and stinging, welled in her eyes. Her vision blurred. She dropped the broom, got into her car, turned the key. The engine turned over, caught. She started to weep. Their first date had been in a car, sharing a six-pack in a Pontiac when she was a cashier at the Big Y and Jerry stocked shelves. They'd been together ever since. She'd never known a life without Jerry. "How am I going to live without you?" she whimpered. "Oh, God, how am I going to live without you?"

She blinked, forcing the tears out, clearing her sight. Why hadn't he listened to her mother? "Jerry," she'd tell him, "now, when you go to a big fire, do one thing: stay back." It was only a joke, but why didn't he listen?

She burst in the front door. The baby-sitter was on the phone, talking to Michelle's mother. Michelle told her she didn't know anything, that she had to use the phone. She called Ralph, then her sister Elaine, and her sister-in-law, Noreen. They all said they were on their way. Then she tried to call the fire department. There was no dial tone. She tried another extension. It was dead, too. She tried different jacks. They were all silent. Her phone line had suddenly gone out, and for no apparent reason. She was frantic, unable to reach anyone. She found Jerry's scanner, plugged it in, tried to glean snippets of information from the radio chatter. But there was too much backgound noise. Nothing came in clearly.

Shortly after ten o'clock, Kathy Spencer's phone rang again. Her in-laws were calling from two doors up.

"Kathy," Tom's father told her, "the fire department wants us to go down to St. Stephen's."

"Why?" Kathy was annoyed. St. Stephen's was all the way downtown.

"I don't know. Maybe they want us to make sandwiches."

Make sandwiches? Kathy was more annoyed, almost perturbed. Twelve hours of work, and she had to drag herself out to fold baloney onto white bread? She took a deep breath. A bad fire, the guys would be hungry. Tom's last night. The brotherhood and all. "All right," she said. "I'll come up."

She pulled on a coat, walked out the door and up the street. Her sister-in-law met her on the sidewalk. She looked worried. "Should I bring the kids?" Kathy asked.

"No, no. Leave them. They'll be fine."

Tom's parents were getting into the car. Their faces were grim. Kathy slipped into the backseat with her sister-in-law. They rode in silence for a few blocks.

"So," Kathy finally said. "Is there something you're not telling me?"

A short silence, then all three in unison. "No."

The drive to St. Stephen's took almost fifteen minutes. Kathy stewed most of the way, still aggravated she was being taken away from her kids to make sandwiches. Her father-in-law parked, and Kathy followed him into the building. There were a couple dozen people inside, firemen or their relatives. She didn't recognize all of them, or even most of them.

She saw a familiar face through the crowd. Dave McGrath, a fireman and a friend of Tom's. He walked toward her, but with an odd gait, a mild lurch, as if his legs had atrophied. He held both his hands out, took Kathy's in his.

"Kathy," he said, "I'm so sorry."

She knew Tom was dead.

She stared blankly, stoic. "About what?"

Dave's eyes opened wider, surprised. "Tom's missing. Didn't you know? Mike McNamee's on his way to your house."

Kathy stopped breathing, had to focus, make her lungs inhale. She had one thought. "I left my kids at home alone," she said. "You've got to get me home. You've got to get me home right now."

A twitch in her stomach. Eggplant parmesan. Her face went white. "Dave, I'm gonna throw up."

Dave stepped to one side, gently nudged her in the direction of the bathroom. Kathy ran past him, through the door, into a stall. Her stomach emptied in three heaves.

Then she lay down on the floor, turned her head, let her cheek rest against the concrete. Ammonia burned her nose, the smell of cleaning fluid masking urine. *I've got to get home,* she thought. *I've got to get to my kids.*

The floor felt cool against her face. She didn't want to move. Outside, Tom was dead and her children were alone and a hundred grieving men were waiting to tell her how sorry they were. Her face would be hot, flushed. The floor felt so cool. She could lie there a little longer.

17

THE TRUCKS HAD ALL BEEN PULLED BACK, AWAY FROM THE warehouse, out of range should the walls collapse. They were arranged in a rough semicircle on Franklin and Arctic Streets, the ladders and aerial scopes fully extended, rising above the building and pouring mighty streams down into the flames. Trucks were positioned on Interstate 290, opposite the big words WORCESTER COLD STORAGE AND WAREHOUSE CO., which were still visible through the smoke. With all the nozzles opened, Worcester firemen were dumping nine thousand gallons onto the building every minute. Still, the fire raged on, swallowed the water, spit it out as steam.

The rest of his men were safe. Mike McNamee knew no one else would be lost, that they would maintain defensive positions, wait for the flames to weary, consume whatever fuel was left, then expire. The warehouse wouldn't claim anyone else, not tonight.

Television cameras and newspaper reporters and photographers lingered on the perimeter. The fire had played out live for more than an hour, a legion of sparkies had been monitoring their scanners, and the glow, a shimmering, dusky orange that lit up the sky, had drawn hundreds of onlookers. By now most of the city knew two firemen were missing, and it wouldn't be long before the true and awful number leaked out. Worried wives and frantic relatives had been dialing fire stations since six-thirty, asking first what was burning, then, later, who was missing, if their husbands and brothers and sons were among the lost. Some of them began to gather near the burning warehouse, peering through the smoke and the steam, searching for a familiar face. So many people were begging for information that the department brass decided to gather them at St. Stephen's Church, eight blocks from the fire.

Mike didn't know who had been called, which families were going to be at St. Stephen's. Someone had to go to their homes, notify them in person, tell them they'd probably been widowed before they heard it on television or read it in the morning paper. Department protocol is to send the chaplain and a chief to break the news. But there were so many, more than anyone had ever had the grim foresight to plan for. More than one chief would have to go, and they would still have to enlist local police officers to help. Randy Chavoor offered to go to four homes. Mike agreed to take the other two.

Joanne was with him, watching from the periphery. She'd made it to Grafton Street, just beyond the highway, before she was stopped by a police line. Two firemen, friends for years, recognized her in the crowd, told her Mike was okay, and then told Mike to go see his wife. "You stay with me," he'd said when she hugged him. "I don't know what's going to happen now, but you stay near me."

She had nodded and followed him toward the warehouse, knees weak with relief. *Mike's alive,* she'd thought. And then a second thought. *I hope this wasn't his screwup. Please, God, don't let this have been Mike's mistake.* She felt ashamed, knew it was her Irish-Catholic fatalism taking over, making her think terrible thoughts. She never said it out loud.

Now Mike was next to her again, asking her if she would go to see Jay Lyons's parents, stay with them. Of course she would. She got into a sedan with her husband and another district chief and a fire chaplain from one of the suburbs who'd raced to the scene as soon as he'd heard two men were missing.

They drove west to Mike's neighborhood, Mike taking slow, deep breaths, trying to keep his composure. The chaplain steered around the last curve on Saxon Road and pulled to the curb across from Mike's own house. Mike got out and looked at the white Colonial where Jay had grown up. He cast his eyes up to a window on the second floor. Jay's bedroom.

He remembered the first time he saw Jay. It was the spring of 1978, a few months after Mike and Joanne had moved in. Mike was in the backyard with Kate, who was just past her second birthday, holding her hand while she toddled along the edge of the lawn near the scrub brush and a small stand of trees. He'd heard a snap in the wood, like a twig breaking or a rabbit disturbing a cluster of dry leaves. Then, from his left, he heard a muffled poof, a burp of compressed air. Another snap in the woods, this one closer to the lawn. Mike looked across the street, squinting a little, his eyes crawling over the front of the Lyonses' house. The barrel of a gun poked from an upstairs window. *Poof. Snap.*

"Come on, Katie," he said to his daughter. "Let's move way over there, on the other side of the yard."

A few days later, Mike had been puttering in his driveway when he saw Jay in person. Skinny little fellow. "Hey, kid," he'd said, loudly enough to be heard across the street. "C'mere."

Jay had dutifully crossed the street. "Yes, sir?"

"You gotta BB gun, right? I want to talk to you about it."

"Um . . . okay." Jay shuffled his feet, squirmed a little, bashful.

"You almost hit my daughter. And me."

Jay squirmed some more, ashamed now.

"Oh, jeez, I'm sorry, mister. I didn't see you, really. I'm sorry."

"Yeah?" Mike eyed him. "Well, what the hell were you shooting at?"

"Just some squirrels I could see from the window. Really." Jay looked up at Mike, stopped fidgeting. "I'm sorry, I really am. I didn't see you."

Mike had considered that for a moment. "Well, all right," he said finally. "But don't do it again."

He hadn't stayed mad at Jay. They ended up talking about the fire department, Jay asking a hundred questions, Mike answering them all. He liked the kid, his enthusiasm. Over the years, as Jay grew into a man, they became friends, equals, no longer a grown-up being nice to the little boy across the street.

Mike lowered his eyes, looked at the lawn, still green in early December. Some afternoons, Jay would stride across that same patch of grass and wave at Mike in his driveway. It was a signal they'd worked out: a wave meant he didn't have time to talk, or nothing to talk about. More often than not, he'd cross Saxon Road. Mike and Jay had most of their important conversations in his driveway. That's where Mike had told him to go be a state trooper, at least try it because he had nothing to lose and where, after Jay had lost everything, he told him to research the civil service rules to see if an ex-con could get his job back with the fire department. He'd listened to him rant about Sully, about how timid he seemed, how he wouldn't let Jay charge through every wall of fire that sprang up on their shift, and Mike had told him to slow down, be patient, that his time would come, that someday there'd be enough fire to go around, enough fire for everyone.

The storm door opened with a creak. Mike saw Joan Lyons, Jay's mother, standing on the stoop. He walked toward her, forcing his feet to keep moving, not feeling them. He stopped on the brick walk.

Joan held the door open with one hand. She kept her other arm pulled close around her waist. "Michael," she said, her voice quaking. "Do you have bad news for me?"

Mike started to answer. He realized she'd never called him Michael before. Always Mike, never formal. The words stuck in his throat. He swallowed, braced himself. "Joan," he whispered, "Jay's missing."

Her knees buckled, her chest convulsed, her face seemed to melt. A reflex pushed Mike forward, up the stairs. He caught her, wrapped his arms around her. He led her inside, gently, almost carrying her. No one else was home. Jay's father, Jim, had already left for St. Stephen's, hoping to hear some word about his only son.

"I have to call Kathy," Joan said. Kathy was Jay's big sister, six years older. "I have to tell Kathy."

"Okay," Mike said softly. "We'll call Kathy. C'mon, we'll call her now."

He followed her into the kitchen, stroking her back as she picked up the phone. Joan stabbed at the keypad with a trembling finger. She hit the wrong buttons. She hung up and started again. Her hands were shaking too badly to dial.

"Here," Mike said, reaching around her, taking the receiver. "I'll call Kathy. Tell me the number, and I'll call her."

She recited seven digits, which Mike pressed. His mind flashed back precisely two years, to December 3, 1997, the night he dialed his own sisters' phone numbers to tell them their father was dead, killed when his car crashed into the back of a tractor trailer. His own fingers had trembled then. Those were the worst calls he'd ever had to make, and, for two years, he had believed they always would be.

Michelle Lucey couldn't get a dial tone. The scanner was gibber-ish, a racket of static and growling. She believed her husband was missing, feared he was dead. But until someone told her, stood in front of her and said the words, maybe it wasn't true. No one on the news had mentioned Jerry Lucey, and no offi-cers' cars had pulled into her driveway. No news was madden-ing but at least it wasn't bad news.

Her brother and sister and sister-in-law stayed with her, waiting for some word, any word. The house began to feel crowded, claustrophobic. Ralph, her brother, said he was going out for some air.

"All right," Michelle said. "Just don't tell me there's a chief's car out there."

Michelle felt her body tense as Ralph opened the door and stepped onto the stoop. She held her breath. But Ralph didn't say anything. The driveway was empty.

She paced. She tried the phones again, fiddled with the scanner. Ten minutes passed.

"Jesus Christ! Oh, Jesus!"

It was Ralph, outside, briefly backlit by the headlights of Randy Chavoor's Expedition. Michelle felt her face flush and her hands go clammy. She knew why they were there.

She saw Randy get out. Paul LaRochelle was with him. Both men started toward the house, Randy slightly ahead. Paul put his hand on the chief's shoulder, slowed him down. "No one's telling Michelle but me," he said.

Randy nodded, let Paul go first.

He didn't have to say anything. Michelle was waiting, eyes wet with tears. They held each other, and then Michelle pulled away, just far enough so she could look at Paul's face, into his eyes. "It's because you weren't with him," she said. She managed a weak smile, then collapsed into tears.

linda McGuirk put Emily to bed, tucked the covers around her, bent down and kissed her on the forehead. Worry creased Emily's face.

"Why can't Daddy call us?" she asked. It was nine o'clock. Joe always called home about then to say goodnight to his wife and children.

Linda sat on the edge of Emily's bed, leaned in closer, brushed a delicate strand of chestnut hair from her daughter's forehead. "Oh, sweetie, I know he wants to," she said. "But he can't right now. There's a really bad fire and he can't get to the phone right now. But he'll be here in the morning."

That seemed to satisfy Emily. Linda leaned over and kissed her again, smiled at her. "Go to sleep," she said. Then she got up and left the room, pulling the door almost closed behind her.

She'd managed to mask her own fear, hide it from Emily. Linda knew Joe would be all right. She'd seen Sully, watched him walk across her television screen. For all Joe's complaining, Sully was a good lieutenant, cautious, by the book. That's who Joe needed looking after him, especially on a night like this.

Truth of it was, Joe liked Sully, off-duty anyway. He'd just ripped out his kitchen for him, was getting ready to put in a new one. And Joe had noticed something else Sully and Jay had in common, besides their smarts. Both of them had a hard time with some of the other guys, Sully because of his officer's swagger, Jay because of his history. Joe was just coming on the department when Jay was reappointed, and he heard the grousing around the station. Firefighting jobs were hard to come by, and a lot of guys thought a disgraced cop and ex-con didn't deserve the privilege. Jay could handle himself all right, though. "Hey, you don't fucking like it?" he'd snap if someone said anything to his face. "Tough shit. I'm here. Deal with it." But Sully and Jay, in their own ways, were both underdogs. Joe liked underdogs. He'd spent seventeen years trying to get on a fire truck. Joe could empathize with underdogs.

But Linda couldn't shake a bad feeling. She thought about putting her pajamas on, curling up in front of the television. A rogue hunch told her not to, that she should stay dressed, just in case she had to go somewhere in a hurry. There were other men to worry about, Joe's friends. The brotherhood. And a relative, Joe's nephew Jimmy. He was on the job. She hoped someone was looking after him.

The phone rang again a few minutes after nine. It had been ringing all night, friends and relatives and people she barely knew, like Joe's high school classmates she'd just met a week ago at his twentieth reunion. She'd bought a new suit for the occasion, dark blue and neatly tailored; two decades and two children hadn't done any damage to her figure. Everyone who called asked the same questions, wanted to know if Joe was on duty, if he was all right, if she'd heard anything. They all had the same tone, cushioned their words with the same sympathetic inflection, as if they were offering condolences, just in case. All that comforting made her uneasy, put her on edge. She gritted her teeth on the third ring. "Stop calling," she said out loud. "Stop calling, because it you keep calling, it's going to be true. You're going to make it true."

A neighbor dropped by, a woman who lived up the street. Her son was a volunteer fireman. She thought she knew what Linda would be going through, wanted to sit with her, keep her company. Her friend Nancy and her sister-in-law Joan both called to say they were on their way. *If I ever need friends in a crisis*, Linda thought, *I'll be all set. But there's not going to be a crisis.*

Linda monitored the newscasts. The toll had climbed, six men were missing. Linda felt a chill. The reporters didn't give any names. Department officials were still notifying relatives.

She looked at the clock. It was almost ten. The evacuation signal had been sounded two hours earlier. She calculated the driving time from downtown Worcester to Rochdale, adding thirty minutes for confusion and traffic. If Joe was missing, there should have been a knock on her door at about 9:10. She added again, trying to account for six families. Another forty minutes. Someone would have been there by now.

The doorbell rang. She froze, afraid to move. Her insides felt as if they'd collapsed again, shattered into fragments that lay in her belly. She went to the door. The knob was slippery in her palm. She pulled it open and saw a local police officer, a friend of the family. He was tipping backward, losing his footing, as if he might tumble off the stoop.

The officer balanced himself, shuffled forward. He was crying.

Linda put a hand to her mouth. "Oh, no," she whimpered. "No . . ."

The cop stepped past her. Emily had gotten out of bed and was standing in the front hall. He swept her up in his arms and cradled her, his own tears moistening the little girl's nightgown.

Mike McNamee saw Tommy Spencer's face again. He concentrated, studied his features, the triangular jaw line, the aquiline nose. He looked into Tom's eyes, only this time in memory. They were clear, irritated by the smoke but focused, set with determination, almost stern. Maybe there was a trace of fear, and there should have been because Tom Spencer knew two men were dying in the boiling fog above him. But there was no hesitation, no reluctance.

Mike replayed the last frames in his head. *I need you to go to the fifth floor.* Tom nodding, strapping his mask in place, then disappearing into the blackness. *Patrick. Daniel. Casey. I know his kids.*

What was he going to tell them now?

He'd left Joanne with Joan Lyons, put them both in a police cruiser to pick up Kathy Lyons and ferry the three of them to St. Stephen's. Then he'd gotten back into the chaplain's car for the ride across the city to Tom Spencer's house. Mike's stomach felt like lead. He was still shaken from telling Joan Lyons that her only son was missing. A man couldn't train for such a moment, couldn't practice how to crush someone softly, how to make two words—"Jay's missing"—any less terrible, less lethal. And he never would have practiced anyway because it never occurred to him that he would have to say something so awful.

He got out of the car slowly, his body aching and exhausted and stiff. He was still wearing his bunker pants and boots, but he'd taken off his coat, stripped down to a dark blue sweatshirt, but he was still perspiring in the forty-degree air. He'd sketched out only the roughest plan. He would go to the door. Kathy, who would have heard him pull up, would be waiting, frightened. And he would say . . . well, he didn't know exactly.

The front door banged open, startled Mike, jerked his attention toward the house. Patrick, Tom and Kathy's oldest, charged out, sprinted down the walk in his stocking feet. "Mike, where's my dad? Where's my dad, Mike, where's my dad?"

Mike held his hands out, slowed Patrick by putting one on each shoulder, held him in position. "Patrick . . ." He took another deep breath, started again. "Patrick, you're dad's missing," he said. "And five other men."

He stared at Patrick, reading his eyes. They were blank, disbelieving. "Patrick," he repeated, softer this time, "your dad's missing."

Patrick collapsed, every muscle liquefying, his body pouring onto Mike's shoulders. Mike grabbed him, felt the boy's chest heave once, then erupt into violent, sobbing spasms. Mike had to take a step back, spread his feet, regain his balance. He held on to Patrick, gripped him until he could breathe again, until the spasms gave way to trembling. Over Patrick's shoulder, on the front stoop, Mike saw Casey standing alone, her arms wrapped tightly to her sides, as if she was trying to hold herself together, keep her body from physically splitting. She was shrieking. It sounded like *No! No!*, but primal, a deep, wounded wail.

A man couldn't practice for that. Mike couldn't even cry, he was so numbed with grief.

It took a few minutes to calm the kids and find out that neither Kathy nor Daniel was home. He would have to be picked up from the party he was at.

"Patrick," Mike said, "do you want me to tell Daniel?"

Patrick shook his head. "No," he said. "I'll tell him. It's something I have to do."

Mike put a hand on his shoulder. Tom would be proud, he thought, his boy stepping up, already trying to be the man of family. "You're sure?" Mike said.

"Yeah," Patrick said. "I'm sure."

Mike pulled the cop aside. "Listen," he said. "Don't let them see the warehouse. I don't care what you have to do, if you've got to go ten miles out of the way. Do not let them see that building."

Denise Brotherton was still wearing her nurse's scrubs, pacing the kitchen. A dozen people hovered around her, neighbors and friends and relatives, keeping vigil. Denise's best friend, Kim, had been there for an hour. Kim suspected the worst. She had happened to be on the phone at about nine o'clock with Paul

LaRochelle's wife, who'd told her, "Kim, hang up the phone right now and get over to Denise's house."

"What are you saying?" Kim asked.

"Listen to me: hang up the phone and get over to Denise's. Now."

Every few minutes, someone would ask Denise if she wanted to go into town, to the warehouse or St. Stephen's. Each time, she said no, repeated what she'd told Paul's cousin. "Paul always told me, 'If anything happens the fire department will come to the house.' This is where I need to be."

She thought about the other Kim, her sister-in-law, eight months pregnant. Kim was at a wedding in Spencer. She probably had no idea about the fire, no frantic fear that her brother, the man who raised her and walked her down the aisle and wanted to coach her through delivery, might be missing or wounded or dead. Which was a good and merciful thing, because all the dread and worry would come to nothing. Paul was alive. Denise believed that, repeated it to herself, over and over, like a mantra or a prayer, clung to it with the same fierce faith she'd always had in Paul, in the two of them. It had been there in the beginning, that night at Tammany Hall, a faith that was blind and irrational and magnificent.

They hadn't been on a date. Denise just felt sorry for him. Paul was an orderly at Worcester City Hospital where she was a nurse, and he'd watched his father die from a cancer that ate away his esophagus, a slow and miserable wasting that finally ended in the spring of 1983. Taking him out for a night on the town was only meant to cheer him up, take his mind off his grief, and it was supposed to be a group endeavour, fourteen other nurses and orderlies tagging along. But everyone else had canceled, leaving just the two of them to drink beer around a sticky table in a smoky nightclub.

She remembered only fragments, disconnected details.

Walking through the carved wooden door to Tammany Hall. Sitting in the shadows of a corner. Her voice hoarse from talking over the blues band on the stage in the back. Paul telling her how smart he thought she was, how he'd always been attracted to intelligent women. Toying with the engagement ring on her finger. Her fiancé's voice whispering through her memory, telling her to quit her job before she met another man and fell in love. Wondering how mad her father would be if she asked him to eat the deposit he'd put down on the reception hall for her wedding.

Everything had happened so quickly after that. A week later, Paul and Denise both broke off their engagements. They were on separate phones at opposite ends of the nursing station on the fourth floor of Worcester City, their fiancés on the line, both of them taking grief about some such thing or another. Paul had caught Denise's attention, rolled his eyes, then held up his index finger and mouthed a silent syllable. *One.*

Denise held up the first two fingers on her left hand. *Two.*

They each raised a third finger. *Three.* On cue, in perfect synchronicity, they hung up the phones.

Three weeks after that night at Tammany Hall, Paul had proposed in a roadside restaurant. The other diners clapped and the manager sent over a bottle of champagne. Then Paul's mother died and Kim was orphaned and life was suddenly enormously complicated and grave and no one would have blamed her if she'd simply walked away but she didn't because she believed in Paul and believed in the two of them together. It had always troubled her that Helen Brotherton had died so abruptly, before Denise knew if her mother-in-law would like her. "She did," Paul would tell her. "I know she did. Because if she didn't, she would have stuck around longer. But she knew her little girl would be in good hands."

Paul believed, too. He accepted the responsibilities that had been thrust upon him. There were times when Denise had been awed by Paul's devotion. When her father was dying in the autumn of 1988, Paul bathed him and shaved him and emptied his catheter. "You shouldn't have to go through that," he told Denise. "There's no reason for you to see your father like that." And he looked after her grandfather, gambled with him at a casino in Connecticut, told him to keep it a secret when they snuck off to a strip-joint called the Lamplighter for lunch. Grandpa was ninety-six years old. Paul thought he should enjoy the time he had left.

Denise grabbed a beer from the refrigerator, popped it open, took a long pull. Something to calm her nerves. She knew everyone who came to wait with her meant well, but the crowd was making her uneasy, as if they had preassembled for the mourning.

She walked from the kitchen, paused at the glass doors that opened onto the deck. Paul had built the deck for her. She'd decided one summer Tuesday that she'd like to have some friends over for a barbecue the following Saturday and, by the way, wouldn't it be nice if they had a deck on which to entertain? Paul dug the holes for the posts that afternoon, cemented them in place on Wednesday, hammered together the frame on Thursday, laid the deck boards on Friday and Saturday. Paul would do anything for Denise.

The family room was opposite the kitchen. Paul's room, big and airy, with skylights cut through a vaulted ceiling to let in the sun. Paul did all the interior work, the wiring, sheetrocking, and finish. A professional carpenter had framed it, a man named Bill Riggieri. They'd gotten to be friends, Bill and Paul, and Bill hired him whenever he needed an extra set of hands. That's where Paul had been that morning, working for Bill out in Shrewsbury.

Denise took another sip from her beer. She was dying for a cigarette. She slipped out the door to the garage, lit one up. Paul and Denise always snuck their smokes in the garage, out of sight of the boys. They called it the GiGi Lounge, which was the name of a bar on the cruise ship that floated them around the Caribbean the year before, their first vacation in years. She didn't know when they would be able to afford another one. Until then, they could pretend in the garage.

It was ten o'clock. The news was on the television in the corner of the family room, where Paul had rebuilt his mangled thumb playing video games with his sons. Worcester Cold Storage roared on the screen, flames shooting up from the roof, engines and aerials spraying impotent streams into the heat. The anchor announced the official toll, six men missing. "All the families," she said, "have been notified."

Denise exhaled, a deep sigh, all of her muscles uncoiling at once. There had been no knock at her door, no chief's car in her driveway. Paul was okay. He'd gotten out. She closed her eyes, leaned her head back, let a wave of relief wash over her.

She heard the purr of engines in front of the house, the soft squeak of brakes, then a car door slam. She snapped her head forward, eyes wide now. She sucked in a short breath, her chest and stomach clenching. She looked at her friend Kim. "Well," she said, "I guess I'm the sixth."

Actually, Mary Jackson ended up being the sixth. At ten o'clock, she didn't know anything was burning, that anyone was lost. Hopedale was twenty-five miles south of Worcester, too far away to be able to see the rusty glow of the flames reflecting off the winter sky or smell the bitter smoke drifting on the wind. And she'd been out all evening, so she hadn't been near a television or a radio, either. She was happy, even smiling when she made the turn off Mendon Street at her yellow bungalow, Tim's blue spruces standing in the front yard like sentries.

She'd had a fine day. She spent the afternoon Christmas shopping with Tim at a mall near the Rhode Island line. They stayed longer than they'd meant to, running far enough behind schedule that they wouldn't have time to brew their regular four o'clock pot of coffee before Tim would have to leave for the station. They stopped at a Dunkin' Donuts instead, got two cups to go, and sat in the car, talking and sipping through plastic lids.

They drove home and Tim hurried to get ready. He told Mary, "I'll see you in the morning," gave her a quick hug and a kiss, and went out the back door. Tim always kissed her good-bye and hello. He expected it and went into a playful pout if he didn't get it right away. In the morning, she knew, he'd come through the back door, kick off his shoes and put on the slippers he kept in the foyer. "Honey, I'm home," he'd say, only exaggerated and goofy, like it was a line from a sitcom. And then he'd linger near the door, waiting for his kiss.

After Tim left, Mary went back out to pick up some small gifts for him. She'd already bought him six videotapes of a public-television series on gardens. She could imagine him sitting in the family room, birch logs burning in the fieldstone fireplace while, outside, snow drifted against the pergola where the yellow roses would bud in the spring, watching hollyhocks and hibiscus bloom across the television screen. Six tapes would carry him through the worst of the winter. She also decided that Tim needed a second pair of slippers, one that he could wear in the house and another for when he wandered his greening yard. After all, it defeated the point of wearing slippers in the house if he was tromping through the mud in the same pair.

She got home at quarter past ten. There were several messages on her answering machine, all of them asking if Tim was working, all of them sounding worried. That struck her as odd. Mary never worried about Tim when he went to work, if only because she had no idea what, precisely, he did. She knew the general outlines, that he'd been on the job for twenty-seven years, that he used to work Rescue 1 before he transferred to Ladder 2, where the pace was slightly slower. But he never gave her any details. He gave her a hint once, pointing up to the roof of a burned-out triple-decker, showing her where he'd chopped a hole through the shingles. "All the way up *there*?" Mary had said. "And you think this is *easier* than rescue?" Other than that, though, he sheltered her from the dodgier realities of firefighting, and even the stylized Hollywood version, like *Backdraft.* "You don't need to see that," he'd told her more than once. When he worked nights, he always had the same report for Mary the next morning when she asked how his shift went. "Long and hard," he'd say with staged weariness.

"Tell me about it."

"I don't even want to talk about it," he'd say.

Mary would flash a knowing smile. "You slept all night, didn't you?"

Tim would nod. It didn't matter if he'd waged a six-hour firefight or drank coffee in front of the TV. "Yeah," he would tell her. "It was pretty quiet."

Mary played back the messages on her answering machine, then turned on the television. The warehouse fire was on all the newscasts, reporters announcing six men were missing and that all the families had been notified and that most of them were gathering at St. Stephen's. She was horrified and relieved at the same time; a terrible tragedy, yes, but no one had notified her. Tim must be all right.

She called Grove Street. No one would tell her anything, only that there was a fire, that Tim had been part of the team fighting it.

"Okay," she said. "Well, tell him I called, and have him call me on my cell phone."

She grabbed her phone and her keys and got back in her car, figuring she could find out more at St. Stephen's, maybe offer some comfort. She pulled onto Mendon Street, turned the wheel toward Worcester, pressed down on the accelerator. Her cell phone chirped before she crossed the border out of Hopedale.

It was Randy Chavoor. "Mary, where are you?"

"I'm driving in," she said. "I'm on my way to St. Stephen's."

"Go home. Please, turn around and go home," Randy said. "We'll come and get you."

She gripped the wheel harder with the one hand that was on it. *Why do they have to come and get me? Why can't I drive in?* She took her foot off the gas, slowed the car. "What's wrong?" she said, her voice cracking.

"Mary, just go home. We'll be there in a few minutes."

"What's wrong?"

"Mary. Please. Go home."

She turned around, drove back along Mendon Street, turned into the access road to the Hopedale Village Cemetery, which led to her driveway. Her pulse was racing, and her hands trembled as she opened the door. She was inside for only a couple minutes when the phone rang. Her daughter, Diane, was calling from her home in Pennsylvania.

"Is Tim working?" she asked. Word of the fire was spreading across the country, by word of mouth—Diane's sister-in-law had called her husband from Worcester—and now by microwaves and satellite uplinks.

"Yes," Mary said.

"Is he all right?"

"I . . . I don't know," Mary said.

Diane could hear the fear in her mother's voice. She absorbed it, started to panic. She was an adult when Tim and Mary met, already married and the mother of a newborn son, but over the past fourteen years she'd come to consider Tim as more of a father than Mary's first husband, who'd moved out when she was a teenager. To her children—she'd given birth to a daughter in 1990—he was Papa Tim, the grandfather who came to dance recitals and built birdhouses and ran through the sprinkler on the lawn on hot summer days and played Santa Claus for Amanda's Brownie troop. Tim always reminded Diane of Santa, the same ruddy cheeks and twinkling eyes, only not as fat. Maybe he would dress up again this year when he came to visit for Christmas. He'd put in for the vacation days, but hadn't told Mary yet. It was going to be a surprise, spending the holiday with Diane and the grandkids.

Mary could hear heavy footsteps outside. Randy Chavoor was at the door. Mary could see it in his face, his eyes moist and sad. She was being notified, just like they said on television. She dropped the phone. Diane heard it hit the floor.

After he watched Patrick Spencer ride off in a police cruiser, Mike McNamee went to St. Stephen's. He had to pay his respects to the families and the other men, offer whatever token of comfort that he could muster. He knew there was nothing he could say, but he had to show up. It had been his fire, his operation, his men. He belonged with them.

The room at the church was crowded with off-duty firemen and their wives, all of them clustering around the families of the missing men, Kathy, Michelle, Linda, Mary, and Jim and Joan Lyons. The mayor was there, as well as the city manager, and Chief Dennis Budd had just finished explaining how awful the night had been. In a weary voice, he told them, "We hold very little hope."

Mike walked through the door just as Budd was finishing. He scanned the room. He spotted Denise Brotherton, sitting in a chair by herself, her skin pale and ashen against her wrinkled blue scrubs.

He went to her, got down on his knees, a supplicant, took

both her hands in his. He didn't say anything, just let Denise stare down at him for a moment.

She spoke first. "Mike, Paul always comes home," she said. "Tell me he's coming home tomorrow."

Mike blinked, instinctively holding back tears. He realized his eyes were dry, that he didn't have any emotions left in reserve. "Denise," he said, "I'm sorry. I can't tell you that."

Denise held his gaze. She seemed to be pleading with her eyes, but her voice was composed. "Mike, I have six sons," she said. "Please tell me he's coming home. Please."

Mike squeezed her hands, looked away, then back again. "I can't, Denise," he said. "I'm sorry, but I can't."

18

THE DELUGE CONTINUED INTO THE NIGHT, GREAT FOUNTAINS OF water arcing from the nozzles on the aerial scopes and ladder trucks and showering down on Worcester Cold Storage. The flames were aggressive, belligerent, as if they'd been emboldened by having forced mortal men to flee for their lives. They feasted on the innards of the warehouse, chewed through the massive timbers and joists that held each floor in place, melted the cork and polystyrene, consumed the partition walls and scraps of trash. Once the fire had pierced the roof, burned wide and ragged holes through the tar and the asphalt, it was able to inhale more oxygen, blow it back out bright and hot.

Mike stood on the street at midnight, after he'd told Joan Lyons her boy was missing and Patrick Spencer his dad was lost and Denise Brotherton he was sorry. He watched the fire rage through smudgy spectacles. A black rain mizzled from the sky, droplets of ash that had risen on clouds of steam and liquefied particles of insulation and roofing, all of it mixing into a charcoal mist that speckled Mike's coat, his helmet, his eyeglasses.

He didn't have to be there. Most of his men, the guys who had fought the initial stages of the battle, had been pulled out, relieved by fresh troops and sent back to their stations to rest and grieve. Counselors were waiting for them, fellow firefighters and psychologists who specialized in disaster, to talk to anyone who wanted or needed their help. Mike didn't want to talk to anyone, not then. There was nothing he wanted to say, nothing he wanted to hear. What could anyone tell him anyway? That it wasn't his fault? That six men—good men, *his* men— choked to death because they had lousy luck or because God was in a particularly vengeful mood that evening or because, the worst thing of all, sometimes bad shit just happened? That he hadn't made a mistake, that there was nothing else he could have done, no decision he should have made sooner or later or differently? That it just wasn't his fucking fault? Would anyone say that? Would it matter? And would he believe it?

Mike wiped his glasses, smeared the soot, put them back on the bridge of his nose. He glowered at the warehouse. *The Building from Hell,* he thought, as if it were the demonic villain in a low-budget thriller. "You've got them in there," he muttered, talking under his breath, cursing the building as if it were alive. "You've got six guys in there."

The night rumbled, a concussion pulsing through the warehouse. Embers and sparks exploded into the sky, cascaded over the walls, fell to the street like fireworks, and the flames leapt higher, glowed more brightly. Mike guessed that one of the floors had collapsed, the impact throwing the cinders into the air, the rush of fresh air fanning the fire like a giant, clumsy bellows. He was fifty yards from the building, across Franklin Street in a parking lot where Car 3, his Expedition, had been stationed as a makeshift command post, yet he could feel the heat, a gust of warm wind that drove the temperature into the eighties.

Mike watched the men arrayed around the building. He saw firefighters from Paxton, Millbury, and Boston, men in blue windbreakers with "ATF"—for the Bureau of Alcohol, Tobacco, and Firearms—stenciled in yellow on the back. The night strobed with red, white, and blue, the lights from fire trucks and, farther out, police cars blocking the nearby streets, diverting traffic from the area. A mile or so to the west, out of view, state police troopers parked their gray and blue Crown Victorias across the eastbound lanes of Interstate 290, blocking traffic. In the lot opposite the warehouse was a van from the state medical examiner's office in Boston. Mike knew there would be six body bags inside.

He replayed the night in his head. It came back to him in shards of memory, each clear and precise, but out of sequence, disjointed. The view from the highway, pale smoke drifting lazily from the roof. Flames swirling toward the elevator shaft. Three identical doors on the third floor. The plunge into darkness. Sully in front of him. *I can't find Jay and Joe.* Calling in the second alarm, being cautious, gathering reinforcements before he needed them. Paul Brotherton on the radio. *Mayday, mayday!* The shriek over the phone when he told Kathy Lyons her brother was missing. Jimmy Pijus behind him. *We couldn't make the third floor.* All those men in front of him, angry, bewildered, horrified, screaming. *They're still up there, goddamnit!*

He held that moment in sharp focus, examined it, dissected it. He'd been lucid, he was sure of that. It occurred to him that he hadn't been scared, that he'd been almost calm. The most awful decision he had ever been forced to make—one fogged by loyalty and responsibility and honor and tradition and unimaginable distress—had been wholly pragmatic. He remembered his words, the blunt declaration. *We've already lost six. We're not going to lose any more.*

Another concussion shook the warehouse. More sparks raced up to the sky, soaring two hundred feet above the streets, and the flames leaped again. A second floor had collapsed. Mike looked toward the warehouse, felt the hot wind blow into his face, watched the water spray into the fire, then rise out as steam.

No man could survive that, he thought, not inside, crawling blind, trying to feel his way out. If he'd sent anyone else in, if he'd let even one of those men push past him, charge into the boiling black, he'd be dead. He had been right to call it off, order everyone out. He was sure of it.

Paul Brotherton was not dead. He was only missing. If the building was as complicated as it had been described to her, a maze of storage rooms and walk-in freezers, Denise reasoned, then Paul could have found refuge behind a thick wall, or squirmed into an air pocket in the debris. People, ordinary people who weren't as skilled or as brave or as resourceful as a fireman on Worcester's Rescue 1, had survived beneath the rubble of an earthquake for days, a week, sometimes longer. Yes, she told herself, Paul was missing but he was alive and he would be when the other firemen, his brothers, dug him out in the morning.

Paul was dead. Denise was sure of it now. He'd run out of air in the belly of an inferno, and when a man could breathe only searing poison, he dies. It was an immutable law of physiology. She had been a nurse long enough to know how it had happened, too. His death had been relatively painless, or it should have been. The smoke would have scorched his throat, but it would have only hurt for a minute, until the carbon monoxide polluted his bloodstream, addled his brain, rendered him mercifully unconscious.

But she could be wrong. She thought of the earthquake survivors again, limp and dusty, rescuers lifting them from a mountain of shattered concrete. Their wives had believed those men were dead, and they'd been wrong. Denise could be wrong. Until they pulled a dead man from the ruins of Worcester Cold Storage, she could hope she was wrong. Her six sons, Paul's six sons, could hope, too.

Three of the boys were awake when she got home. It was one-thirty in the morning and there were people in the house, friends and relatives, all talking nervously, some of them crying. The boys asked their mother what was going on.

"There's a really bad fire, guys," she said. "And . . ." And what? Daddy's dead? Daddy's missing? Daddy's trapped under smoldering bricks waiting to be dug out? She didn't know, which is what she told them. "It's a really bad one. I don't know if Daddy's going to be able to beat this one."

Mike, the oldest, didn't say a word, just turned and walked away. Brian threw up. Timothy, nine years old, the fourth son, simply wept.

The warehouse was still burning at dawn, heaving lead-gray smoke up against the morning's flat silver sky. The worst had passed, the towering flames finally beaten back, the fuel inside depleted and soggy. But the fire was stubborn, refusing to completely surrender.

No one had been able to get back inside since Randy Chavoor had crawled out just after eight o'clock the night before. The ferocious heat and smoke that had forced the men to retreat had done tremendous damage to the interior, burning away the supports, weakening the entire structure. After almost a century of squatting on the edge of downtown like a square-edged mountain, sturdy and solid, Worcester Cold Storage was now a fragile shell.

Firemen knew that the danger did not end when the flames had been extinguished. Floors weakened, walls buckled, roofs sagged. Charred ruins were inherently treacherous, unstable jumbles that could crush a man as surely as fire could burn him and smoke could choke him. The deadliest firefighting disaster in New England, in fact, had happened after the flames went out. On June 17, 1972, Boston firemen spent three hours snuffing a four-alarm fire at the old Hotel Vendome. They were prowling the wreckage afterward when part of the building collapsed, crushing nine men to death.

The Worcester chiefs weren't taking any more chances with the warehouse, wouldn't give it an opportunity to kill anyone else. A crane was ordered to the scene to begin dismantling the exterior walls, knock at least one of them down, split the building open so they could see what they were up against.

The crane was positioned on Arctic Street, near the stairwell where Mike had sent men up to search for Paul and Jerry. It was a huge machine, a long steel spire dangling a thick cable, on the end of which was a 4,500-pound wrecking ball. Mike stood off to one side, far enough away from the building that he wouldn't be caught in an avalanche of bricks and mortar. The crane operator hauled the ball into the air, raised it almost to the top of the wall. He shifted his levers, swung the ball away, then back toward the warehouse.

Mike heard a dull thud, felt a vibration beneath his feet. But the wall held. A puff of mortar dust marked where the ball had struck, but no bricks fell.

He turned to look at the man running the crane. The operator opened his eyes wide, exaggerated surprise, then shook his head. The building was tougher than it appeared. It seemed malevolent, deliberately frustrating the puny men who challenged it. Most of Group II, the shift that had been on duty when the warehouse began to burn, had returned to the scene. Hundreds of other firemen—from Worcester, Boston, and a dozen other cities and towns—were there, too, all of them desperate to get inside, to start searching. Like Denise and the other wives, they held on to a slim hope that someone had survived. Even if all six were dead—which every man knew in his gut was the truth—they needed to recover the bodies, retrieve them from the ashes. Firemen never left a brother behind.

The wrecking ball swung again. Another thud, but no noticeable damage. On the third strike, a handful of chips snapped off the brick facing and fluttered to the ground. Mike kicked the pavement with the toe of his boot in frustration.

As the day wore on, the big ball taking small chunks from the B wall, the rest of the men were growing restless, tense and edgy. They milled around the staging area in the parking lot across Franklin Street, next to a blue tent that had been set up to shelter the families of the missing six. Emotions were raw. Men bickered, sniped at each other. A rumor circulated that firefighters from out of town would be sent into the building first, that Worcester men wouldn't be able to bring out their own. More loud voices, angry shouting.

Mike set up a stepladder, climbed to the third rung so he could see the entire crowd, holler down on them. "Hey," he barked. The men quieted. "Now listen to me. We've never been through something like this before. . . ."

Grumbling from the men, their voices rising again.

"Hey! Listen. We're going to get through this. But now is not the time to be fighting. We're all doing the best we can here."

He scanned their tired faces. Hardly any of them had slept for more than an hour, and most not even that long. They were still caked in sweat and cinders. Some of them had feared for their lives only hours before, had been certain they were going to die, right there, right then. And they wanted to go back in. Mike understood how they felt. He wanted to get inside.

By late afternoon, the wrecking ball had hammered a rough V shape through the B wall, making it seem as if the bricks were being slowly unzipped. From Arctic Street, Mike and the rest of the men got their first clear view of the inside. The floors had indeed collapsed, pancaking one on top of the other. The second floor had apparently held, though it was hard to be certain from that angle. The rubble from the upper floors was piled more than twenty feet deep. Finding the bottom would take days of digging.

The men could also see the fire wall, opposite of and parallel to the side the crane was dismantling. From the doorways cut into it and the holes that had once held the charred stubs of floor joists, they could count exactly how many levels the warehouse had contained. Six, which meant Paul and Jerry had been lost on the fifth floor, two down from the roof. At least they'd looked in the right place.

A team of searchers ventured onto the pile shortly before dusk. They did only a surface scan at first, carefully picking their way through the smoldering debris, looking for any sign of movement, any trace of the missing six. Spot fires flared, and flames still crackled from behind the firewall.

Mike was exhausted, but he remained on his feet, patrolling the grounds, picking through the ruins. He wondered if he might be in shock, if the enormity of the fire, of the loss, had overloaded his emotions. He hadn't shed a tear or thrashed in a rage. Six men down. It didn't seem real. He was too close to it, surrounded by it. From his position on Franklin Street, he couldn't see the grief rippling outward, through the city, across the state, into the wider world.

The streets nearby were crowded with pedestrians who stared at the gray ribbons of smoke puffing into the air. They were hushed and somber, not morbid gawkers come to rubberneck the gore but more like mourners come to pay their respects on hallowed ground. Gov. Paul Cellucci ordered all state flags to be flown at half-mast. At most of the fire stations in the commonwealth, the flags were lowered as a matter of course. Pres.

Bill Clinton wrote a letter of condolence, which was printed in the local paper:

> Hillary and I were deeply saddened to learn of the tragedy that has struck the Worcester community. The six firefighters, who are now missing and presumed dead, valiantly put their lives on the line in the effort to save others and protect their city. Their courageous service reminds us all of the tremendous commitment and sacrifice made by the thousands of firefighters across America who risk their own lives every day to protect our communities.

Ordinary folks sent condolences and cash. An anonymous donor wrote a $10,000 check to the Salvation Army Saturday morning, and by the afternoon, less than twenty-four hours after the first alarm, the *Telegram & Gazette* collected $1,200 for a relief fund the newspaper had established the night before. Eventually, the paper would collect more than $6 million.

The men in the ruins, grimy and tired, didn't know any of that, not then. And they might have been chagrined. Friday night they'd been waiting to eat dinner on secondhand furniture in stations where, not so many years before, they'd been told to keep the doors closed on even the hottest summer nights so testy taxpayers wouldn't see them sitting around, waiting for the bell to go off. Friday night, they sent out trucks with too few men and with radios that shorted out when they got wet. Friday night, they had to borrow a thermal imager from a neighboring town, a piece of equipment that might have helped them see through the smoke, might have saved two men if they'd been able to crawl in with it an hour earlier. Friday night, they had gone into a death trap that had stood vacant for a decade, that was supposed to have been shuttered tight, an aging hulk on a decrepit block in which the Worcester Redevelopment Authority had invested $89,000—the price of three thermal imagers—to study whether a private developer could convert it into a biotech facility. Friday night, Paul and Jerry and Tommy and Tim and Jay and Joe were alive.

Saturday morning, the president was calling them heroes and the governor was in a state of official mourning and people were throwing money at their corpses. It was all well intended, but disquieting just the same.

Darkness fell. Lights were attached to large stands, their beams directed into the warehouse, illuminating the wreckage and the men who scoured it. Mike could feel the fatigue now, his reflexes slowing, his mind blurring. He decided to get some rest, come back early the next morning. From the look of things, there would still be work to do then, enough digging for everyone.

He got home and took a long, hot shower, scrubbing off the filth, trying to wash away all the dirty traces of the night. He thought about the details of the recovery, how cranes and backhoes could do some of the work, but that most of it would have to be done with shovels and sifting screens. He was still thinking like a tactician, professional, focused.

After he dried himself and dressed, he padded through the den and into the living room and eased into an easy chair covered with orange velour, so old that it had molded to his shape. The chair faced the front window. He stared at the Lyonses' house, his mind numb.

The phone rang. He picked it up. "Hello?"

It was Kate, his oldest daughter. "Hi, Daddy."

Mike heard her voice and started to cry. He sat in his chair, facing the window, and wept.

19

MIKE STEERED HIS GOLD BUICK AROUND THE LONG WAY, TO the far end of Franklin Street, avoiding the avenues that the police had blocked off. It was early, about nine o'clock Sunday morning, almost forty hours after the first alarm rang for Worcester Cold Storage. As he drove down a long hill, he could see the warehouse smoldering beneath him, a pall of yellow-gray smoke held low to the ground under an unusually bright December sky. Fire and brimstone, he thought. The Building from Hell.

Joanne sat next to him. She eyed the building, remembered when Mike had told her how badly it scared him. She wondered if it had known, if the warehouse itself was alive and malevolent, if it had been stalking her husband, her friends, all those men. She watched the steam and the smoke pulse out of the ruins. It was breathing, hissing at her. "It's a devil," she muttered. She hardened her glare. "That building's a devil." She decided she would stare it down, stand on the street and watch it finally die.

Mike parked the Buick fifty yards from the warehouse and walked the rest of the way to the command post in the parking lot opposite the A-B corner of the building. He wasn't scheduled to work, and, in his jeans and sweatshirt, he wasn't dressed for it. But he'd been drawn to the building, compelled to be there when his men were finally found. He'd stowed his gear—boots, coat, pants, helmet—in the trunk of the Buick.

Most of the B wall had been torn down and part of the A wall, opening a gaping wound in the corner of the warehouse. He leaned against the chain-link fence, folded his arms across his chest, and stared at the wreckage. The devastation was immense and thorough, an isolated landscape from Dresden or Berlin, something he'd only seen in black-and-white war footage. Charred timbers, big as maples, jutted up at sharp angles through mangled coils of refrigeration piping and tangles of wire and heaps of shattered concrete, all of it covered with slushy cinders. Near the center wall, men played streams of water on spot fires and flare-ups, and the steam hung over the detritus like white flak smoke. And that was only half of it: the rest of the building lay behind the firewall, waiting to be exposed.

They were all dead. Mike had suspected that since Friday night, but now he was certain. The warehouse had become a crematorium, its thick shell holding in the heat, its insides disintegrating, crumbling, melting. For a few deadly hours, the building had functioned like the woodstove in his kitchen, air flowing into a combustion chamber, alchemizing into fire, exhausting through the chimney. Yet the destruction was contained in the firebox, a controlled burn that never spread to the counters or the china hutch. When the logs had been consumed, Mike swept out the ash. His men would be sweeping ash from Worcester Cold Storage.

He watched a dozen men scramble across the jumble on the deck, which is what the second floor, where the others had collapsed, was called. The search for bodies was a deliberate process, conducted in carefully organized phases to both preserve any evidence of arson and to retrieve human remains. After the two exterior walls had been pulled down, the men divided the deck into sections. They did a surface search first, walking through the debris, stepping around beams and loose bricks, scanning for a hose, a helmet, a badge, anything that might reveal a body. Then cranes lifted away the largest pieces of wreckage and deposited them on Franklin Street. After another surface search, the loose material was scooped out with a clamshell bucket and piled in the street. Firemen raked through the mounds, picking out the larger pieces, spreading the rest out to look for clues and remains. The smaller fragments were sifted through a screen of half-inch mesh and, finally, quarter-inch mesh.

It was filthy and miserable work, picking through wet ashes and warm bricks under a raw December sky. The men were wet and sore and grieving, and a few were suffering wounds from the firefight on Friday night. Robert A. had sucked in so much smoke, had scarred his throat so badly, that he couldn't speak and wouldn't be able to for another six weeks. Mike Coakley ignored the sharp ache stabbing at his chest, the result of three ribs he'd torn out of place. But every man from the Worcester Fire Department wanted to be on the deck, his fingers blistered and chapped, scraping through the ruins for his comrades. When the crane swung the bucket clear, the officer in charge on the deck would yell "Go!" and every man would scurry across the deck and dig like mad. "Ho!" meant clear the area, that the crane was coming back, that men shouldn't be lingering in its path. Mike noticed no one moved as quickly getting out of the way.

An hour after Mike arrived, a few minutes after ten o'clock, one of the deputy chiefs ambled up to him. "Mike, I hate to do this to you," Walter Giard said. "But we need you. We could really use you up there."

Mike jerked away from the fence. "Absolutely," he said. "I

just didn't know how you wanted to work this, if you wanted the regular shifts working. But I've got my gear in the car."

He turned toward his Buick, took a step. A flicker in his peripheral vision, all the men on the deck converging on a single point, like bees to a hive. He wheeled, sprinted toward the warehouse. "What's going on?" he asked the first man he saw.

"We got one."

Mike ran up Franklin Street, flung open the trunk, kicked off his civilian shoes. He stepped into his bunker pants, rammed his feet into his boots, and started running back toward the warehouse, pulling his coat on between strides, the heavy gear slowing his pace. He went to the B wall, near where the overhead doors were hidden behind the rubble, and hustled up a long yellow ladder that angled up to the deck. The other men were gathered approximately halfway between the remnants of the B wall and the fire wall, but closer to the front, the Franklin Street side. Mike reconstructed the building from memory. The stairwell, the only exit down from the fifth floor, was about thirty feet away. The man they'd found had been only ten big steps away from getting out alive.

Scorched mortar crunched under Mike's boots. He noticed the site had fallen church quiet, the rumbling cranes shut down, the hissing hoses switched off. It was difficult to see the corpse, to separate it from the burnt shards surrounding and partially covering it. Men dug gently, lifting pieces of rubble aside, careful not to disturb the remains more than necessary.

Fire did ugly things to the human body, private things, damage that no one should be forced or maybe even allowed to see. When it was one of their own, privacy was even more important. Below, at the corner of Arctic and Franklin, the aluminum ladder from the back of Tommy Spencer's truck, Ladder 2, slowly extended into the air. Three men climbed out on it with massive tarps. They draped them over the stick, secured them with rope, let them hang in the still and smoky air like a giant curtain, blocking the view into the warehouse.

It took fifteen minutes to untangle the body from the debris. Up close, seeing how big the man was, most of the men guessed they'd found Tim Jackson.

A body bag and a stretcher were brought to the deck. The remains were freed, then tenderly packed into the black plastic bag. District Chief Larry Mulry blinked back tears as the bag was placed on the stretcher. "No," he said. "He's not going down in that fucking body bag. No one's going to see him like that."

Worcester firemen had no protocol for recovering their own dead. They were improvising, cribbing from terrible scenes they'd witnessed somewhere else, Boston, New York, and Chicago. But no one argued with Chief Mulry. The men waited on the deck, behind the drape hanging from Ladder 2, until a red firehouse blanket was brought up to cover Tim's body. Then four men from his station, Grove Street, lifted the stretcher and carried it toward the B wall. Mike walked in front, leading the procession. At the edge of the deck, a second ladder had been placed parallel to the first, and firemen from Grove Street and Central Street passed the stretcher to the ground.

At the bottom, the rest of the firemen, paramedics, and police officers stood in two lines, forming a corridor that led from the base of the warehouse to the ambulance. A reverend waited partway down the line to say a prayer over the body. Then Mike led them to the ambulance, where the men slid the stretcher inside.

From the moment his body had been found, only Worcester firemen touched Timmy Jackson's body.

For hours, the search focused in the same area, the clamshell bucket closing, rising, swinging away, men monkeying back to the dig site. There should have been another body nearby. Firemen worked in pairs, would have clung to each other in the dark. But there was no one else beneath that particular mound of debris. Tim might have become separated from Tom Spencer in the roaring black. Or he might have died somewhere else, closer to the fire wall or more toward the center of the building, and his corpse slid to its eventual position as each of the floors collapsed. No one knew, had any way of knowing. So they dug deeper, through ten feet of debris.

Mike stayed on the deck through most of the morning and into the afternoon. An hour or so before dusk, he climbed down to Franklin Street to rest. Near the fence surrounding the parking lot across the street, he saw one of the men from the Fire Investigations Unit.

"You guys got any idea how this started?" Mike asked the investigator.

He looked to either side, made sure no civilians or reporters were within earshot. "Yeah," he said quietly. "We got two people, and we got confessions from both of them. But keep it quiet. We aren't releasing it yet."

Mike nodded. He had only one question. "Was it intentional?"

The investigator shook his head. "No," he said. "It doesn't appear so."

Finding Tom Levesque and Julie Ann Barnes hadn't taken long. Early Friday night, before the evacuation signal was sounded, two detectives from the Worcester Police Department's arson squad, Michael Sabatalo and Michael Mulvey, canvassed the bystanders and onlookers, ferreting out witnesses. One of the people they spoke to was Bill McNeil, who ran an all-night diner called Bill's Place on the corner of Franklin and Grafton streets, on the other side of the highway from Worcester Cold Storage. Bill had told the police early on that homeless people lived in the warehouse; by Saturday morning, he was wracked with guilt, convinced—wrongly—that none of the firemen would have gone into the building if he'd kept his mouth shut. For the next week, he fed any man who asked for free.

When the detectives came to see him Friday night, Bill gave them two names: Tom Levesque, who he'd hired to wash dishes for a few weeks the previous summer, and Julie Ann Barnes. Sabatalo and Mulvey found them both the following morning, Saturday, and, in separate interviews, they both told essentially the same story. Tom had wanted to have sex, they argued, then struggled, a candle tipped, the fire spread, they left. The only difference was what time all that had happened. Tom said about four-thirty, but Julie thought it was about six o'clock.

They weren't arrested right away, though, and hadn't been by Sunday afternoon. The detectives were still building their case. They talked to Scott, a man Julie dated for a few weeks in September. He confirmed that Tom and Julie had lived in the warehouse, and described the squalid office where they kept their bed, the heater, and the candles. They talked to Bruce, with whom Julie was staying in room 410 at the Regency Suites Hotel in Main South. He knew about the fire because the window in his room faced the orange glow searing the sky above the highway. He said that Julie watched the fire with him.

Mike listened to the rough outlines of the story. "Son of a bitch," he muttered. Maybe it would have been better if the building had been torched, if an arsonist had lit it up for insurance or revenge. Then there would have been a villain, a bona fide criminal, a murderer. There would have been someone to blame. Instead, there was only a pair of vagrants, pathetic, almost pitiable. He could imagine them, unwashed and disheveled, tussling amid the filth in the warehouse. If they'd reported it earlier, if Tom was right and the fire had burned for almost two hours before the first alarm rang, would it have made a difference? Mike was sure it would have. But the worst thing they'd done was run away. Mike couldn't help but wonder whether six of his men were dead because two misfits were too scared to dial 911.

He shook his head as he walked away. "Son of a bitch," he said again. "What a stupid, stupid thing."

Emily McGuirk understood why her daddy couldn't come home yet. She had figured out exactly what had happened and she wasn't happy about it but she understood and she was very proud of her father.

She knew there had been a bad fire in a warehouse and that her father had gone into the building with his friend Jay Lyons. When they were inside, Jay got hurt. Her father would never leave his friend alone, especially if he was hurt. So that's why he hadn't come home. He was in the warehouse, next to Jay, waiting for the other firemen to dig them free.

Joe McGuirk had been gone a long time, though, almost four days. Emily hadn't seen her father since she kissed him at the bottom of the stairs on Friday afternoon. Her mother had let her sleep with her and Everett every night, the three of them curled together in Linda's bed. That helped a little. But she was still upset.

"I'm so worried about Daddy," she told her mom on Tuesday. "Because now he's missed breakfast and lunch and dinner and breakfast and lunch and dinner and breakfast and lunch and dinner and breakfast. That's"—she counted, added everything up—"four breakfasts and three lunches and three dinners."

Linda hugged her daughter, pulled her close. "I know," she whispered in her ear. "I'm worried about Daddy, too."

When the sun went down, banks of heavy-duty lights threw a lunar-white shine across the deck. The timbers and coils and men broke the light, cast strange shadows onto the rubble and the remnants of the walls. The searching continued around the clock, all through the night, stopping only once, before dawn on Monday, when it appeared the firewall might topple down, eighty feet of bricks and mortar crashing onto the deck. The digging started again the next morning, after a giant crane removed the wall.

Five men were still missing. There had been no other body near Tim Jackson. Two dogs, trained to find cadavers, prowled the ruins now, their snouts low, near the ash, sniffing. Every so often, one of them would loiter over a certain spot, then take a step backward and sit, the signal that she had smelled something human. The men would focus on that area, scooping with small hand trowels and their fingers. But they found only bits of canvas hose, nozzles, scraps of leather, items that had only been touched by humans. After almost three days of painstaking excavation, the men were increasingly frustrated. Yet they still jockeyed for shifts on the deck. No one wanted to quit.

Tom Levesque and Julie Ann Barnes were in jail. They'd been picked up that day, Tuesday, and arraigned earlier in the afternoon on six counts each of involuntary manslaughter. They shuffled into a courtroom only a half mile from the warehouse, Levesque gaunt and scruffy, briefly lifting his hands to shield his face, then dropping them, realizing the gesture was futile or uncomfortable or both. Barnes stood close by his side, her mouth drooping into a defeated frown, a white ribbon knotted in her mousy brown hair. They were being charged under the legally vaporous theory that their failure to report the fire made them criminally responsible for the deaths of six men. Under Massachusetts law, however, that wasn't necessarily a crime. After pleading not guilty, the judge set bail at one million dollars each. Barnes was sent to the state prison for women in Framingham, which was standard for female prisoners, and Levesque was shipped to the Middlesex County Jail in Cambridge, which was not at all standard. But it was safer. Worcester is a small city; too many jail guards knew at least one of the six dead firemen.

At the warehouse, no one celebrated the arrests. Nothing had changed. Like Mike McNamee, most of the firemen were more frustrated than angry. Chief Dennis Budd spoke for most of them when he told the local paper he wasn't seething with rage. "I have no time for that," he said. "I feel grief right now." Paul Brotherton and Jerry Lucey went deep into the building because conditions allowed it and that was their job. Maybe the building wouldn't have turned so deadly so quickly if Levesque or Barnes had called earlier. Or maybe it would have. And Tom Spencer, Tim Jackson, Jay Lyons, and Joe McGuirk still would have gone in to find Paul and Jerry. Now they had to get them out, bring their brothers home.

The search area had shifted forward, toward the Franklin Street side, and about twenty more feet toward the fire wall, into one of the worst sections of the building. When the fire was at its zenith, state police hovered above in a helicopter with a device that measured the temperatures below. Where the men were digging had been one of the hottest spots, soaring to more than 3,000 degrees. Bodies are cremated at 1,800. Cast iron melts at 2,800. Everything in the front of Worcester Cold Storage should have been vaporized.

Then they found something. Just before eight o'clock, a hand went up, waved everyone over. Some pieces of equipment, the outer gear. Men got down on their knees and dug, determined and rapid but still delicate, precise, none of them wanting to overlook anything important.

Bricks were lifted aside. Ashes and cinders and crumbled cork were trowled away, inch by inch. A glint of silver through the sludge. A medallion, the size of a quarter, with pieces of a fine-looped chain attached to it. An icon of St. Florian, the words stamped into the metal: PROTECT US.

They'd found Jay Lyons. His medallion was sterling silver, which has a melting point of 1,600 degrees. Every man there knew what St. Florian had told his tormentors. *If you burn me, I will climb to heaven on the flames.*

And in the cold of a December night, they believed it was true.

20

LINDA McGUIRK'S EYES FLUTTERED OPEN IN THE DARK BEFORE dawn on Thursday morning. She'd slept only a couple of hours, and then only fitfully. The emotional strain of the past six days were exacting a physical toll. She'd hardly eaten since last Friday night's dinner, grief and exhaustion sapping her appetite.

She knew Thursday was going to be a long day. The memorial service for Joe and the other five men—organized by the International Association of Firefighters—was scheduled for later in the morning, and it seemed like the whole world had shown up for it. Thirty-thousand firefighters, from Anchorage, Los Angeles, Boise, Montreal, Australia, Ireland, and all over the commonwealth, had come to the city to march down Main Street and into the Worcester Centrum Centre, where the bishop would recite a prayer and President Clinton would say a few soothing words. Television cameras would carry it live.

The cameras had been there all week, beaming pictures of the smoldering warehouse and weary firemen and teary bystanders across the planet. Since Saturday morning, a disaster in a small city in the middle of Massachusetts had been a national tragedy, an occasion for public grieving and official mourning.

It was touching in a way, strangers from Hawaii and New York and South Carolina sending cards, flowers, and money, almost a million dollars already to the *Telegram & Gazette*'s fund. Yet it was disconcerting, too, the attention, the sense that Linda's most awful moments were not, could not, be private. She'd been to the warehouse only once, the day after, and she'd left as soon as the impromptu press conference began. Everett had thrown up all the way home, and every time she pulled to the side of the road for him, Linda worried a photographer might take his picture, print an image of a distraught widow and her vomiting son in the newspaper.

A limousine would be there by eight o'clock to take Linda and her children and everyone else to the Centrum. Linda's own mother, Ann Howe, had been staying with her, and Eddie Ryan, a firefighter who was her liaison to the department, was there as well. They would help her get the kids ready. And they would keep the press away, shield her as best they could from the cameras and the microphones.

She felt Emily curled next to her in the bed. She was warm, almost hot. Linda reached for Emily's hands. She could always judge a fever in her children by feeling their hands. Emily's were burning. Her temperature had to be more than one hundred degrees. She gently shook her, tried to rouse her. Emily softly murmured and opened her eyes. They were glassy, another symptom Linda had learned to recognize. Emily was too sick to get out of bed, let alone leave the house.

Linda wrapped her arms around her daughter. She heard a knock on the door, then her mother telling her it was time to get up.

"I'm not going," Linda said. "Emily's sick."

"You have to go."

"No, I don't." She pulled Emily closer. "I can't leave Emily."

"Linda, come on. I'll stay with Emily. You really have to go. The president's going to be there."

"I don't give a shit," Linda snapped. "I don't even like Clinton."

"But . . ."

Eddie Ryan appeared in the doorway. He and Linda's mother tag-teamed her, both of them pleading with her to go, convincing her Emily would be all right, reminding her that Clinton, Sen. Edward M. Kennedy, the bishop, and thousands of Joe's brother firefighters had come to honor her husband. She had to go, had to accept their sympathies, allow them to mourn with her.

She relented after a bit, protested again when she couldn't knot the necktie that went with Everett's new suit. Eddie tied it for him. Then she had to dress herself. She decided to wear the same tailored outfit she'd worn to Joe's twentieth high school reunion less than a month before.

The clothes slipped off, the jacket sliding from her thin shoulders. It didn't fit anymore. In six days, Linda had lost fourteen pounds.

With safety pins and her mother's help, Linda managed to get the suit to fit, or at least stay in place. She was ready when the limo arrived. She stroked Emily's forehead, told her she'd be home as soon as she could, then kissed her goodbye.

The procession began in Chadwick Square, a few blocks beyond the Grove Street station, an army of firefighters assembling in close-order ranks, their dress uniforms pressed and starched, black elastic bands stretched around their badges. If Jerry Lucey hadn't switched trucks Friday night, if it had been another man missing in the warehouse, he would have been in front, in the first line with the Worcester Fire Department color guard. Just two years earlier, he'd marched down Commonwealth Avenue in Boston for the dedication of the memorial to Boston men who had died in the collapse of the Hotel Vendome. And Jay Lyons, if he'd practiced for a few more months, would have been behind him in one of the seven rows of firemen playing bagpipes and drums, all of them dressed in green plaid kilts. He was going to surprise his mother once he'd mastered the pipes.

The color guard marched south on Grove Street, past the station where Jay had driven Engine 3 out of its bay, where Tom Spencer had been working his last night on Ladder 2 with Tim Jackson. They walked a mile to Main Street, the dirge of pipes and drums behind them, then another half mile to Central Street, where they turned left. A block farther, in the street between Central Station and the Centrum, they stepped under an arch formed by the ladders rising from two Worcester trucks straddling the street, a massive American flag hanging from the apex. Civilians, twenty thousand of them, lined the route, standing seven and eight deep. The firefighters manning the stations stood at attention, some on trucks pulled to the curb. None of them was from Worcester. They were from Marblehead and Fall River and Leominster and other Massachusetts towns, volunteering so Worcester men could mourn their own.

The memorial service was scheduled to begin at eleven o'clock, but firefighters continued to stream around the corner of Main and Central for nearly another hour, a river of dress blues broken by small pools of Gaelic plaid and color-guard flags. Five minutes before noon, the last of the marchers—firefighters from Buffalo, New York, and Bayonne, New Jersey, and, finally, a solitary flag-bearer from the American Legion—passed beneath the outstretched ladders and the flag.

The Centrum only held about fifteen thousand people, barely the headwaters of the firefighters rippling through downtown. They trickled into the arena, row by row, Worcester firemen taking the seats arranged in the middle of the floor, the others filling the mezzanine and balconies. The remainder of the procession, another fifteen thousand firefighters and even more civilians, filled the streets outside, where loudspeakers had been mounted to broadcast the ceremony inside.

Just before eleven-thirty, Denise Brotherton and three of her sons were escorted into the arena by Worcester fireman Mike Conley. The Centrum fell silent except for the rustle of all those starched uniforms, everyone rising at once, standing at attention. Denise felt the eyes upon her. The aisle blurred. Her feet tingled.

"Oh, no," she whispered to her liaison as she gripped the crook of his elbow more tightly. "I think I'm going to pass out."

Mike patted her hand. "Dear," he whispered back, "I don't think that would be a very good idea right now."

Denise stifled a small laugh, felt her head clear, her nerves calm. She glanced back at her sons. All of them wore Rescue 1 sweatshirts.

The other five families followed, each led by a Worcester fireman to seats in the front row. The clergy, union officials, and politicians filed onto the stage, in front of which stood sprays of white lilies and snapdragons and poster-size photos of Paul, Jerry, Tom, Tim, Jay, and Joe.

At 11:34, the Most Reverend Daniel Reilly, the bishop of Worcester, strode to the podium to begin a long program of eulogies and hymns and sad poems. Eleven men spoke. Gov. Paul Cellucci compared the missing to World War II veterans. Ted Kennedy read "May They Not Be Forgotten," twenty-eight lines by an anonymous author that begin with, "Brother when you weep for me, remember that it was meant to be." Frank Raffa, the president of the local chapter of the International Association of Fire Fighters, could barely speak the names of the six dead men, the words catching on a lump in his throat. More than ninety minutes and three renditions of "Amazing Grace" passed before Rep. James McGovern introduced Bill Clinton, who quoted Isaiah and the Book of Kings and Benjamin Franklin.

Firefighters wept in the balcony. Michelle dabbed at her eyes with a tissue and stroked her oldest son's shoulder. Patrick Spencer kept his arm around his mother. The Lyons family, Jim, Joan, and Jay's sister, Kathy, held each other in a tight embrace.

But it was too much for a little boy who'd lost his father six days before. Sitting in the front row with Everett, Linda was almost relieved that Emily wasn't there. Everett had yet to shed a tear, held everything inside, close and deep. His grief came out instead in a spastic tic. His head snapped back and forth, sharp quick nods, and his throat choked out a guttural grunt. He couldn't control it. Linda could only pull his head onto her shoulder, hold it there, caress his temple until he quieted. As the ceremony wore on, the snapping and grunting increased. By the time Sen. John Kerry presented the families with flags that had flown over the Capitol on December 3, she only wanted to get him home. When two state troopers began to play taps, she leaned over and whispered in his ear. "We'll be out of here, soon," she said. "Just a few more minutes."

At home, Emily's fever was already breaking. Later that night, Linda would thank Joe for visiting his daughter in the night, making her just a little warm, warm enough to stay in bed.

Franklin Street was quiet except for a doleful trumpet sounding taps through a loudspeaker. Twenty men who'd been working the deck all morning stood at attention, somber, respectful. As the final note faded, they returned to the pile of rubble, sifting through ashes in the street, climbing over the wreckage on the deck.

They had taken a few breaks during the morning, pausing to watch moments of the memorial service on jumbo monitors that had been set up at the site. Every so often, the faces of the men who'd died, the men they were digging out of the ruins, hovered above them on the screens, electronic ghosts. The images—Tim Jackson smiling on a spring day beneath the pergola where his yellow roses grew; Jerry Lucey in his dress uniform, his eyebrows, arched thick and black beneath his white cap, giving him a look of mild surprise; Jay Lyons with his head cocked, laughing—slowed the men, as if the great weight of the tragedy had become physically real. But only briefly. They all seemed to dig faster in the minutes that followed.

The past thirty-six hours had been frustrating, an endless and wearying process of scooping and sifting that had turned up no trace of the four missing men. After they found Jay, the men had hoped Joe McGuirk would be nearby, that they had stayed together inside the warehouse. Apparently, they hadn't. There was a possibility that Jay had gotten badly lost, that he'd died alone. Or he had switched partners in the dark, hooking up with Tim, their bodies being separated only when the floors collapsed. That would have most likely meant Joe was with Tom Spencer. But they hadn't found him, either.

The deck was mostly cleared between the B wall and the firewall, which was being whacked apart by a wrecking ball. Beyond it, the other half of the building was covered with ten feet of debris. Somewhere inside, small fires still burned, coughed a haze of gray-white smoke into the sky, a cloud that drifted over the interstate toward the Centrum.

The dig continued into the night under the glare of the lights, then into the next morning, progressing foot by foot beyond the firewall. On Friday afternoon, one of the men sifting broken bricks and ash through a screen of quarter-inch mesh found Tim

Jackson's wedding ring, a plain gold band with Mary's name etched inside. Tim was being waked that day. Mary would have his ring back before the funeral.

The wreckage was being removed from front to rear, the clamshell bucket and the men working in a wide swath from Franklin Street in. Progress was maddeningly slow. As darkness fell on Friday, they were a quarter of the way in, just short of where the only door between the two sides of the building had been. The lights came on, the crane hauled away another load, men scrambled back with shovels and trowels and bare hands. After eight more hours, they'd pushed to the doorway. At one-thirty on Saturday morning, a few feet farther in and next to the remnants of the firewall, they found Joe and Tom Spencer. Their bodies were close, as if they'd groped through the door-way together. They must have been horribly disoriented, mov-ing in the wrong direction, away from the stairwell that would have led them to the ground.

Jerry was found next, five hours later, just as dawn was breaking. His body was near the D wall, far back from Franklin Street, almost in the rear corner of the warehouse behind the elevator shaft. When the building filled with smoke and visibil-ity was cut to zero, he and Paul were as far away as possible from the stairs, sequestered behind a thick wall that muffled the squeal of their PASS alarms. No one could've heard them, let alone found them. Mike Coakley had been right: by the time Paul and Jerry had radioed mayday, they were already dying.

Denise Brotherton heard about Jerry being found from a television newscast early that afternoon. The hope she'd clung to a week earlier had faded, ebbing a little each day. Now that Jerry was dead, now that there was a corpse, she knew Paul was, too. And he would be near Jerry. She wanted to be there when they brought him out.

She was at the site by two-thirty. She spent most of the afternoon in a blue tent next to the freeway that had been set up for the families, part of a camp of mess halls and cots that had been erected over the past week. All day long, firemen came off the deck to hug her, the soot from their turnout gear smudging her white coat to black. They told her how sorry they were, that they were close, that it wouldn't be much longer.

Day stretched into evening. Denise stood out on the street, watching the shadows from the work lights play across the D wall. She noticed a flicker of orange high above the deck. A piece of cork, still clinging to the bricks, had caught fire. *Well, at least it's keeping Paul warm,* she thought. She considered that, repeated it in her head, then quietly chortled at herself. *Yeah, like Paul needs to be kept warm.*

Up on the deck, one of the dogs sniffed next to the elevator shaft, lingered, then stepped back and sat. One of the men hustled down to Denise. "I think we've got a hit," he told her. "What should we be looking for?"

"Dog tags," Denise said. "Paul always said to look for his dog tags."

Another hour passed. Twenty minutes after nine o'clock, she told one of the men to take a beer up with him. "Put a Sam Adams on the deck," she said. "And just yell, 'Hey, Paul, we've got a Sam up here for you.' He'll hear that." She managed to smile when she said it.

She waited another forty minutes, then saw Chief Budd striding across the pavement. He ushered her into one of the blue tents. There were tears in his eyes. "This is the hardest job I've ever had to do," he said, his voice raspy, hoarse. "But I want you to have these." He laid Paul's dog tags in her hand, gently, as if they were fine and fragile things that might shatter.

It was nearly eleven o'clock when the procession formed around Paul's body. Mike McNamee, who had led the first five men off the deck, wasn't there. He was at home, collapsed in bed, after eight numbing days at the site. Other men from Central Street carried Paul across the deck to the ladders. As they neared the edge, Denise noticed the cork on the wall flare up, the light brighter, hotter. She watched as the men passed Paul's body down to the ground. Then she looked at the cork again, saw it flare a final time high on the wall and then go out, as quickly and quietly as it had ignited.

21

MIKE KICKED THE HARLEY TO LIFE, GAVE THE THROTTLE TWO quick twists, felt the engine rumble. He let the clutch out, puttered to the end of the driveway, turned into the street and accelerated, notching through the gears with his toe. Spring air rushed against his face, cool, almost chilly against his cheeks, a strong wind to blow the stray and dreary thoughts from his mind.

He'd thought of the warehouse that morning. And the night before and the morning before that and on and on, back to the beginning. Sixteen months after Worcester Cold Storage burned, it was still the first thing on his mind when he woke up, the last thing before he went to sleep. If he jerked awake in the quiet dark of his bedroom, well after midnight but long before dawn, he thought of it then, too. Always then. The particular moments were different. Sometimes he was in the stairway and the smoke was pouring down, blinding and choking. Or maybe he saw Tom Spencer's face or heard Paul Brotherton's voice. Sometimes, it happened all over again, only all at once, the hours and minutes compressed into a single snarled memory.

He rode north out of the city, toward the two-lane blacktops that stretched out into the countryside. The sky was a brilliant April blue and the leaves on the maples were young and pale green. He could get lost on a day like that, let the Harley decide which road to follow, leave his own mind idling in neutral for a while. It would help keep him sane.

Mike worked on that a lot, his sanity. Not that he ever thought he was going crazy, but he knew the warehouse fire had changed him, just like it had changed every fireman in Worcester, maybe everyone in the entire city. Each of them dealt with it in his own way. Mike, he was a talker. He gave interviews to newspaper reporters and Dan Rather and spoke at fire conventions and wept with counselors, told everyone who asked the same story, every detail. What he feared the most, more than even another burning warehouse going so bad so fast, was Worcester Cold Storage sneaking up on him, the same building coming after him, rising out of the misty past, strangling him a year or ten or twenty down the line. He wanted to excise all his demons right then.

It was interesting to watch the way different men responded to the same event. Some of them wanted another fire almost immediately, almost as if they feared losing their nerve if they had to sit around waiting, replaying the last one, remembering the minutes when they thought they might die, too. A couple didn't get a choice. Mike Coakley had inhaled so much poison and damaged his lungs so severely that one breath of the wrong toxin could kill him on the spot, only no one could be certain which chemicals would do it. "You're done," the doctor told him. "I'm not done," Coakley said. "I'm a fireman. I'm not leaving." The department forced him to retire anyway.

Some men had to get away, find new surroundings. John Sullivan, who was as brave as any man that night, as brave as any man who had ever sworn the oath, transferred off Engine 3 and into the drill school. Jay used to tease him about how those who couldn't do, taught. After December 3, it wasn't such a funny joke. Tom Dwyer, Paul Brotherton's partner on Rescue 1, transferred to the Grove Street station. Of the nineteen men who'd worked together, practically lived together, on the Group II shift at Central Street, only six would be at the station two years later.

Then there was Joe LeBlanc. Joe was on vacation the night of the fire, but after twenty-four years on the rescue truck he was a wisened veteran, a mentor of sorts to Paul Brotherton. And they were very close, on and off the job. The day before Joe left for his vacation, three weeks before the fire, Paul had hugged him, then kissed him on the cheek. "I love you like a brother, Joe," he'd said. "I love you like a father." Joe heard about the fire while he was on a cruise ship floating in the Caribbean. He was bringing a souvenir home for Paul: two beads he had braided into his short, gray hair to prove he wasn't as uptight as Paul used to insist he was. He left them on Paul's casket. He went back to Rescue 1, but it wasn't the same. The only fires Joe wanted to see anymore were in his living room fireplace on a wintry day. He was counting the months until he could retire.

Mike didn't want to retire. He might want to change a few things, though, maybe get out of the shift command, take a weekday job, something with a regular schedule. There was talk of creating a safety officer, appointing a man to analyze tactics, strategy, and equipment. Mike thought he might be good at that.

The irony could make him shiver if he dwelled on it. Mike had always been a stickler for safety, always trying out new gear, teaching recruits how to protect themselves. Yet in the defining inferno of his career, the one that took six of his men, he wasn't sure what he could have done to protect anyone. Safety ropes would have helped, sure, but the department didn't have them, not long enough to follow Paul and Jerry all the way across the warehouse. The men finally had a few thermal imagers, paid for with donated money, charity from the kindness of strangers.

But would one have helped that night? He wasn't sure. No imager could see through eighteen inches of brick.

No one else seemed to have any answers, either. The National Institute for Occupational Safety and Health issued a report on the fire, but other than stating the obvious—that the department needed more and better radios—it offered nothing definitive or particularly constructive. The department had its own Board of Inquiry examine the night minute by minute. The BOI produced a magnificent document, detailed and thorough, but it assigned no blame and found no serious flaws in the attack.

At least there were no longer any questions about how the fire had started. Once the deck had been cleared, arson investigators found evidence—a glob of red wax, the outlines of a pallet used as a mattress, the charred remains of a cat and small dog—that corroborated the statements Levesque and Barnes had given them. Less certain was what would happen to them. A judge had dismissed the manslaughter charges against both of them because there is no law against not reporting a fire in Massachusetts. The district attorney was appealing, trying to get the charges reinstated. It had just been in the paper last week. Mike wasn't sure how he felt about that. Sometimes he almost felt sorry for Barnes, retarded and pregnant and living in squalor. She was in Maine now, taken in by the same couple who'd raised her little sister since she was a toddler. They'd recognized Julie from her picture in the newspapers, raised her bail money, took her north to live. They were trying to adopt her, make it official, and eventually would. That had been in the papers, too. It got a little tiresome, though, reading about her happy new life.

He had hoped that December 3, 2000, the first anniversary, would bring some type of closure, though he wasn't sure how such an amorphous concept would materialize. Maybe it was just a milestone that would push the demarcation of his adult life a little farther into his past, nudge it out of his present. For a full twelve months, the city had lived with The Fire. Because the events had played out in public, flickering on television screens for eight agonizing days, the public insisted on grieving with people who, before their husbands and fathers and friends were killed, had been quite private citizens. The widows were recognized in airports and restaurants and shopping malls. There were banquets and fund-raisers and plaques presented before the crowds at professional sporting events, all of which were very sincere and graciously and gratefully accepted. Yet Worcester firemen, and especially the families of the six Fallen Heroes, as they'd come to be known, were celebrity mourners. It is difficult to truly grieve when strangers are watching.

Mike thought of Jim Lyons. Jim was fascinated by the attention. He pondered it for months, wondering why he had crates of cards and letters from all over the country, why people would stop him on the street and say they were honored to meet him. "Did you hear that, Joan?" he'd ask every time it happened. "Honored. He was *honored* to meet me."

But it wasn't so difficult to figure out. On a sweltering summer day eight months after he'd died, Jay's name, along with those of the other five Worcester firemen, was carved into a granite monument in Colorado Springs. The International Association of Fire Fighters' Fallen Firefighter Memorial is etched with hundreds of names, men who were either killed on the job or years later by the lingering, malignant residue of soot, smoke, and heat. There is a similar monument in Emmitsburg, Maryland, and in most every town, and certainly every big city, there are granite markers and bronze plaques etched with the names of firemen who didn't survive a local fire. When a firefighter dies, he is not simply grieved; he is revered as a martyr. And if dying on the job makes a man a martyr, then simply showing up for work every day makes him a hero. There was an elegant logic to it all, a nobility that seemed to comfort him.

Mike leaned into a curve on the outskirts of Paxton, a bucolic little town just over the city line, then straightened onto the ribbon of road stretched out before him. The Harley felt good, handled well. A good-looking bike, too, a 1995 Heritage Softail, black on charcoal. It used to belong to Jay Lyons, was his prize possession, until one day in the spring of 2000 when Jim Lyons wheeled it across the street and gave it to Mike. He said he thought Jay would have wanted him to have it. Mike fought back tears as he accepted. He thought, *They don't blame me.*

No one blamed Mike. A lot of people, all of his men, actually considered him a hero. He stood at the foot of a staircase that led into a cauldron of black poison, facing men blinded by desperation and determination, and said, "No more." If he'd let them, every man there would have gone back up. Some of them, maybe most of them, wouldn't have come back down. He had the courage to admit defeat, and to men who had never lost before.

Mike knew from the beginning that it hadn't been his fault. Yet he didn't believe it, not in his guts where it mattered. Even now, roaring past new-budding fields sixteen months later, he could have a flash of doubt, start to dissect the night, replay each frame, search again for anything he could have done differently, should have done differently. He never found anything, though, and he looked less and less with each passing week.

He opened the throttle, let the staccato pop of the engine bounce around inside his helmet. Then something caught his eye in the western sky. A black column, twisting against the blue like knotted strands of yarn. He watched it for miles, all the way into North Brookfield, the smoke beginning to mushroom, flatten out and spread. Small orange slashes appeared just above the horizon, tendrils of fire snapping upward.

It was closer now, perhaps five miles away. From behind, over the growl of his bike, he heard the wail of sirens. He glanced in the mirror: two tanker trucks, loaded with water, lights flashing, barreled up the road. He steered to the side, gave them a wide berth, but maintained his speed. He couldn't see what was burning, but it had to be huge; a black cloud loomed above like a thunderhead. Mike kept riding toward it, by habit or perhaps even instinct, the proverbial moth to the literal flames.

He crossed the line into Hardwick. An old mill had caught fire, a spectacular blaze, at least four alarms on its way to five. A shot of adrenaline hit his bloodstream. He twisted the throttle harder.

Then he stopped. He backed off the accelerator, pulled to the side of the road, cut the engine. The fire was only a half mile away. He could smell it, almost taste the smoke. He looked behind him, blue sky over green buds, an asphalt ribbon laced between them. He looked forward. Black and orange. He kicked the engine over, revved it, shook his head and laughed at himself. "What are you doing?" he said out loud. "It's a beautiful day. And you've seen enough of this shit."

He let out the clutch and steered into a looping turn toward home.